Cambridge Elements

Elements in the Philosophy of Biology
edited by
Grant Ramsey
KU Leuven
Michael Ruse
Florida State University

CONTROLLED EXPERIMENTS

Jutta Schickore
Indiana University

CAMBRIDGE
UNIVERSITY PRESS

CAMBRIDGE
UNIVERSITY PRESS

Shaftesbury Road, Cambridge CB2 8EA, United Kingdom

One Liberty Plaza, 20th Floor, New York, NY 10006, USA

477 Williamstown Road, Port Melbourne, VIC 3207, Australia

314–321, 3rd Floor, Plot 3, Splendor Forum, Jasola District Centre, New Delhi – 110025, India

103 Penang Road, #05–06/07, Visioncrest Commercial, Singapore 238467

Cambridge University Press is part of Cambridge University Press & Assessment, a department of the University of Cambridge.

We share the University's mission to contribute to society through the pursuit of education, learning and research at the highest international levels of excellence.

www.cambridge.org
Information on this title: www.cambridge.org/9781009494793

DOI: 10.1017/9781009348966

When citing this work, please include a reference to the DOI 10.1017/9781009348966

First published 2024

A catalogue record for this publication is available from the British Library

ISBN 978-1-009-49479-3 Hardback
ISBN 978-1-009-34893-5 Paperback
ISSN 2515-1126 (online)
ISSN 2515-1118 (print)

Controlled Experiments

Elements in the Philosophy of Biology

DOI: 10.1017/9781009348966
First published online: December 2024

Jutta Schickore
Indiana University

Author for correspondence: Jutta Schickore, jschicko@iu.edu

Abstract: Control is a key ingredient of scientific experimentation; arguably, an uncontrolled intervention or manipulation is not even a genuine experiment. Experiments in the life sciences, however, are notoriously difficult to control due to the complexity and variability of living things. This Element discusses general features of controlled experimentation, epistemic and practical aspects, and historical perspectives. It argues that controlled experimentation has a material-technical and a conceptual side. It shifts the focus from control experiments, comparisons with a control, to the broader issue of controlling for background factors as the epistemologically fundamental issue in experimentation. To understand the nature of controlled experimentation, one needs to consider the making – the design phase – of controlled experiments, particularly the conceptualization and treatment of background factors. The making of controlled experiments is at the same time constitutive for the knowledge that can be gained in the experiment, contingent on a research situation, and historically shaped.

Keywords: control experiment, scientific method, experimental method, confounders, scientific test

ISBNs: 9781009494793 (HB), 9781009348935 (PB), 9781009348966 (OC)
ISSNs: 2515-1126 (online), 2515-1118 (print)

Contents

1 Introduction

In an article published in 2019 in *EMBO Reports* (one of the journals of the European Molecular Biology Organization), the two biomedical researchers John Torday and František Baluška note: "[O]nce we began our formal training as scientists, the greatest challenge beyond formulating a testable or refutable hypothesis was designing appropriate controls for an experiment. In theory, this seems trivial, but in practice, it is often difficult" (Torday and Baluška 2019, 1). This Element exposes the roots of the difficulties, discussing foundational, historical, and pragmatic questions about experimental control.

Scientists attach great significance to experimental control; they equate the process of designing controls with understanding what the experimental intervention does. Arguably, an uncontrolled intervention or manipulation is not even a genuine scientific experiment. An experiment deemed insufficiently controlled is unlikely to be accepted in the scientific community. Scientific articles routinely mention controls; handbooks and instruction manuals on methods and protocols in the life sciences regularly call for the inclusion or setup of control experiments.

According to a recent editorial of *Nature Cell Biology*, evaluating the appropriateness of controls is one of the core elements of successful reviewing. Reviewers should "identify critical weaknesses, suggest experiments to bolster support of the central claims, and comment on the robustness, validity and reliability of data. Feedback on the adequate description of methodology, the appropriateness of experimental design and required controls, the validity of data analyses and statistics, and the quality and reproducibility of data is central in assessing the strength of a manuscript" ("Principles of Refereeing" 2017). Discussions of controls can be found in laboratory manuals or the numerous "protocols" available nowadays, which describe the measures of control that are common in the target field.[1]

The notion of control is as ubiquitous in scientific practice and scientific publications as it is in everyday life. In everyday contexts, the term "control" is associated with oversight, management, check, and constraint. We seek to control passports, pests, riots, or temperatures. "Control" also lends itself to figurative usage; it is tempting to describe a persuasive speaker as one who can control her audiences, for example, or the work of a journal editor in terms of a control mechanism for the communication of content. In scientific contexts, researchers

[1] There is an entire series of manuals just for molecular biology, for example, entitled *Methods in Molecular Biology*, which currently encompasses more than 2,500 titles, with themes ranging from *Proteomic Profiling* to *Plant Cell and Tissue Culture*. The book series is published by a commercial publishing house, Springer, so the high number of volumes in part reflects the economic interest of the publishers. Nevertheless, the number is astounding.

speak of controls, controlled experiments, control experiments, control measurement, positive controls, negative controls, indirect controls, control groups, control animals, randomized controlled trials (RCTs), and so forth.

Despite the fundamental importance that scientists attach to experimental controls, the concept of control is not well understood. Or perhaps it is because experimental control is so pervasive and taken for granted both in science and in everyday contexts that the concept remains elusive. Only few broad analyses of control in experimentation exist. Many systematic and historical questions are wide open, such as: Why is it so challenging to design adequate controls for an experiment? What is a perfectly controlled experiment, and can perfect control ever be achieved in science? Are there universal control setups? What exactly is the difference (if any) between a control experiment and a controlled experiment? Is experimental control an ancient, early modern, or recent feature of scientific inquiry?

This Element discusses common systematic features of and historical perspectives on controlled experimentation. The perspective is pragmatic. The aim is to provide a general framework that is helpful for understanding broader swaths of present-day and past experimental practices.[2] I consider experiments as forms of active inquiry, as interventions done by human agents who seek to gain knowledge about the world. On this view, controlled experiments can be provisionally characterized as interventions deliberately designed such that the effects of the experimental intervention become manifest to the human agent. The following sections develop this idea in more detail.

A pragmatic or practice-oriented approach to philosophy-of-science questions inevitably includes tradeoffs. I do not engage with abstract philosophical points in analytic epistemology and metaphysics that, arguably, are not immediately relevant to understanding the epistemic and practical issues arising in actual scientific practice. This has to do with the method of formal philosophical analysis of key epistemic (or moral, or aesthetic) concepts. One typically proceeds by offering preliminary, general explications in terms of the types of conditions that need to be in place for these concepts to apply. Then, the previously accepted explications are probed by constructing cases that do not fit with those explications and revised accordingly. To advance the conceptual analysis of experimental control, specific examples of the right kind are needed – examples that fit a given general

[2] I am not committed to a particular version of pragmatism here. I use "pragmatic" loosely to indicate an analytic orientation to actual, as opposed to ideal, epistemic situations, procedures, and methodologies. This is in line with recent, and not so recent, work on philosophy of science and epistemology that is anchored in scientific practice and attentive to the historical development of scientific methodologies, such as the works by Ian Hacking (1998), Friedrich Steinle (2005), William Wimsatt (2007), Hasok Chang (2022), or Hans-Jörg Rheinberger (2023), to name only a few.

characterization of "experimental control" but that one would not be inclined to call "control." For the purpose of formal analysis, it is fine and often unavoidable to reconstruct actual episodes from past and present science, to simplify, disambiguate, add features, or even make up examples entirely.[3] By contrast, I examine common, typical scientific practices rather than construed cases. To make the account broadly applicable to actual scientific inquiry, I de-emphasize epistemological ideals and smooth over some conceptual intricacies in current philosophical discussions; instead, I draw out the complexity, uncertainty, and openness of actual experimental practice and possible ways to address them.

The tradeoff will be in evidence throughout this Element. I operate on an understanding of experimentation that is informed by interventionist theories of causation, but my approach is eclectic. I will not discuss current issues in philosophy of causation. (There are two Elements for that!)[4] In fact, in my discussion, I will sometimes use insights drawn from older theories of causation such as John Mackie's and H. L. A. Hart and Tony Honoré's, even though more recent works in philosophy of causality have exposed several shortcomings of these theories. These shortcomings, however, have not been fully overcome, and the modifications that *have* been offered are of limited use for understanding the quotidian experimental practices that are the main topic of this Element. Arguably, the discussions of causation by Mackie and even more so by Hart and Honoré are at the right level of abstractness for my purposes.[5] They address and solve certain problems with classic accounts of causation (especially John Stuart Mill's) while still being attuned to episodes from actual practice.

I use the notions "controlled experiment" and "controlled experimentation" as umbrella terms that refer to all experimentation involving some form of deliberate, organized intervention. I distinguish two main aspects of controlled experimentation. One is the management of experimental target systems and background factors. The other is the comparative experimental strategy or design, whereby a target system or experimental group receiving treatment is compared with a reference target system or group that does not receive treatment. Scientists often use the expression "control for" something when they

[3] Paul Grice characterized the process of conceptual analysis as being "in a position to apply or withhold [the expression] E in particular cases, but to be looking for a general characterization of the types of case in which one would apply E rather than withhold it." Then, one would test this general characterization "by trying to find or imagine a particular situation which fits the suggested characterization and yet would not be a situation in which one would apply E. If one fails, after careful consideration on these lines, to find any such situation, then one is more or less confident that the suggested characterization of the use of E is satisfactory" (1989, 174).

[4] Fenton-Glynn 2021, Pence 2021.

[5] In what follows, I will draw on both. I will not discuss Mackie's main contribution to the philosophy of causation, the INUS condition. While the INUS condition is a key component of Mackie's account, this Element is not primarily concerned with theories of causation.

refer to the management of the target system and background factors, and "control experiment" when they refer to comparative experimental designs. A "control" is the reference case or treatment with which the experimental intervention or treatment is compared. These terms and distinctions will be further clarified in the text.

Experimental control has a material-technical and a conceptual-epistemic side. Experimental control encompasses managing the target system in its setting, the apparatus for intervention, the detector, and residual tools as well as mobilizing knowledge to account for the experimental intervention, the apparatus, and the environment in which the experiment is going on. Examining the making – the design – of controlled experiments is crucial for understanding the nature of controlled experimentation philosophically. What must be controlled, and how, is worked out partly by drawing on tradition, and importantly by second-order experiments. Experimental control is at the same time constitutive for the knowledge that can be gained in the experiment, historically shaped, and contingent on a research situation.

Section 2 introduces three epistemological notions of "perfectly controlled experiment" and their purposes. While these notions specify ideals that are unattainable in actual practice, they usefully pick out two main control issues in scientific inquiry: managing the target system and background and instantiating a comparison to establish a cause–effect relation. Section 3 examines the key component of all controlled experimentation, namely the background against which a controlled intervention on the target system is carried out. The background, it is often said, must be "held fixed" so that the effect of an experimental intervention can become manifest to the experimenter. The section examines this background, its main structural components, and how it is treated, organized, and conceptualized in practice. Section 4 discusses experimental control in historical perspective, using spontaneous generation research as an example. It illustrates how past researchers dealt with control tasks long before the term "control" entered scientific discourse. Section 5 opens up a long-term perspective on control strategies. Section 6 addresses the question of whether there are universal control setups, showing that there are routine ways of controlling in established scientific fields. In situations in which inquirers venture out into new fields, however, it is plausible to say that experiments and control setups emerge together. The section argues that to understand the epistemic significance of experimental control, philosophical analysis needs to attend to the design phase – the making – of controlled experimentation. This process is both a conceptual and a technical process, and a collective one as well. It is constitutive of the knowledge gained in experimentation, and it typically involves experimentation – second-order experimentation. Section 7 draws together the main points of the discussion.

Much of the account presented can be applied to experimentation outside the biomedical sciences. Arguably, however, biological objects pose specific problems for experimental control, and the biomedical sciences have been driving forces for the development of scientific control practices.

What is not covered? There are numerous aspects of control in and of the (life) sciences that this short Element barely touches upon or does not discuss at all. The most notable omissions are ethical regulations of experimental practices; legally significant guidelines for clinical and laboratory practices in the development of a new drug;[6] the possibilities and dangers of controlling the genetic makeup and development of organisms (Pauly 1987, Curry 2016); mathematical and computational forms of control (Cinelli, Forney, and Pearl 2022); the control of data, including statistical controls for different types of errors (e.g. by selecting appropriate confidence levels) and statistical power; epistemological issues concerning RCTs (Worrall 2007, Cartwright 2010, Fuller 2019, Krauss 2021) and the broader cultures of control that have an impact on the sciences. The literature on the last topic is especially vast. Historians and sociologists of science have examined issues such as commercial and legal pressures on biomedical experimentation and historical aspects of the development of RCTs (e.g. Marks 1997, Holman 2020); state surveillance and the advancement of techniques for governing people (e.g. Foucault 1975, Foucault 1979, Gigerenzer et al. 1989, Seppel and Tribe 2017); and institutional and political oversight of scientific data production and restrictions of the flow of scientific information (e.g. Galison 2010). Moreover, this Element does not cover control in the more figurative senses of "controlling scientific or public audiences"[7] or "controlling inferences," that is, using aggregated experimental data to support or reject theoretical hypotheses.[8] I have chosen to focus more

[6] These guidelines comprise the performance of the trials themselves, that is, the operating procedures, control of assay performance, reagents, materials, data, and documentation, but also the organization of the activities, the facility, and the personnel involved. They are issued by organizations like the OECD (OECD Working Party on Good Laboratory Practice 2022) or commercial providers ("A Guide to Good Laboratory Practice (GLP)" (Safety Culture Content Team 2023)). Guidelines also cover the conditions for assay validation to ensure comparability between multiple laboratories (Sarzotti-Kelsoe et al. 2009). One main purpose of such guidelines is to help ensure adequate documentation of data quality as required in courts of law.

[7] As historians and sociologists of science have demonstrated, ultimately, controlling an experiment succeeds only if scientists are able to "control" the audience responses. There are some well-described cases illustrating this point. Antoine Lavoisier famously demonstrated the production of water in combustion with expensive instruments in front of Paris audiences (Lehman and Bensaude-Vincent 2007). In the English world, Robert Boyle relied on machines like the air pump to establish experimental philosophy (Shapin and Schaffer 1985). In each of these cases, well-crafted public experiments played an important role in persuading the community.

[8] A recent example for this approach to control is Miriam Solomon's notion of "validator" (Solomon 2022).

narrowly on epistemic, methodological, pragmatic, and historical aspects of control as they arise in day-to-day experimental inquiry in the life sciences.

2 Perfectly Controlled Experiments and the Pragmatics of Experimental Control

2.1 Restraints and Checks

Philosophical discussions about experimental control (what little there is) have been diverse. There are few distinct philosophical approaches to the topic, and the definitions and characterizations of "control" that have been advanced in various contexts are not easy to reconcile. This is, in part, because some analysts treat the question of experimental control as a methodological one and others as a formal epistemological one. Another reason is that to be able to talk meaningfully about experimental control, we first need to specify what an experiment is, and there is no agreement on this notion either. Moreover, discussions about experimentation and experimental controls lead into other thorny philosophical issues, notably causation, explanation, confirmation, and probability.

A useful starting point for my discussion is Edwin Boring's "The Nature and History of Experimental Control" of 1954. It is one of a few systematic studies of experimental control; at the same time, it illustrates how complex and multifaceted the topic is. Boring distinguished three main meanings of "control" in the context of experimentation: "control" in the sense of "restraint . . . to keep conditions constant"; "control" in the sense of "guidance . . . causing an independent variable to vary in a known and specific manner"; and "control in the general sense of a check or comparison." He added that control as check or comparison "appears in all experimentation because a discoverable fact is a difference or a relation, and a discovered datum has significance only as it is related to a frame of reference, to a relatum" (Boring 1954, 589).[9]

Boring's distinctions range across quite different aspects of experimental control. On the one hand, there is the material-practical aspect of experimentation. Experimentation is an activity, an active intervention in a (material-social) setting in the world by a human either with or without tools or machines, whereby a change is produced. "Experimental control" in the general sense of "restraint" refers to a targeted intervention in an otherwise stable situation whereby a feature of the target system is caused to vary in a specific manner to produce a change, while everything else is held fixed – an act of "maintaining constancy," as Boring put it (Boring 1954, 573). In this sense, control is the distinctive feature of all

[9] He also situated control experiments in the context of nineteenth- and twentieth-century science and philosophy of science, suggesting that John Stuart Mill offered the first philosophical account of experimental control (Boring 1954, 589). I will return to the historical thesis in Sections 4 and 5.

scientific experimentation. It is what distinguishes scientific experimentation from playing, messing around, or aimlessly tinkering with things. On the other hand, there is the epistemic aspect, which is implied in Boring's discussion of controlled intervention. Experimenters make interventions to gain empirical knowledge, and the more they control – restrain – their interventions and the experimental setting, the better they are able to learn what change results from the intervention they made.

Boring also noted that controlled intervention involves a check, a verification, and added the enigmatic phrase "verification restrains." He then went on to explain that "check" meant verification by comparison. The word's original meaning is "*counter-roll* (*contre-rolle*), a duplicate register or account made to verify an official or first-made account and thus a check by a later roll upon the earlier" (Boring 1954, 573). A register is a bureaucratic device to maintain order in some area, and a *duplicate* register is a device to check whether order was maintained appropriately. Here control is considered as a check *on* an intervention to assess whether the intervention did what it was supposed to do, like a duplicate register by which one assesses whether one's accounting was correct.

As Boring's discussion indicates, the notion of control in the context of experimentation is equivocal. Experimentation is both a form of control and depends on control: It is an intervention that one makes to determine what changes result from the manipulation of a factor. Only within a stable, *controlled* setting is it possible to discover the difference that an intervention makes in the setting. In an uncontrolled situation, one is unable, or less able, to do so. In this broad sense, good, epistemically productive experimentation simply *is* controlled experimentation, and the perfectly controlled experiment is the experiment that is best suited to produce empirical knowledge. Control in the context of scientific experimentation also refers to the control *of* the experiment, the procedures to ensure that the intervention was done correctly. In this perspective, control is an assessment *of* the experimental intervention.

In what follows, I will use the term "controlled experimentation" for an experimenter's targeted interventions in a material-social setting in the world in order to gain empirical knowledge. Controlled experimentation comprises the more specific tasks of controlling for background factors and of making control experiments as further explained in what follows. Before I turn to these tasks, I consider the concept "perfectly controlled experiment" and its place in philosophical theories of causation and formal epistemology. As we will see in the next section, different interpretations of "perfectly controlled experiment" have been proposed in the recent philosophical literature.

2.2 Perfectly Controlled Experiments

Angela Potochnik et al.'s recent definition of "perfectly controlled experiment" makes the notion of controlled experimentation (in the sense just specified) more precise. In perfectly controlled experimentation, "experimenters perform an appropriate intervention on an independent variable and then measure the effect of this intervention on the dependent variable. All extraneous variables are fully controlled, so no confounding variables are possible. All changes in the behavior of the system thus must be due to the experimenters' intervention" (Potochnik, Colombo, and Wright 2019, 63). In this definition, as in Boring's explication of controlled experimentation as restraint and guidance, experimentation simply is controlled intervention.

The perfect experiment, the *perfectly controlled* experiment, is understood as a manipulation of a target system whereby all the factors affecting the system are identified and held fixed, except for the intervention on the system. This notion of a perfectly controlled intervention in a fully stabilized situation encompasses the material and practical dimensions of experimentation, the ordering and stabilizing of an experimental arrangement that needs to be in place for experimentation to generate empirical knowledge about cause–effect relations.

At first glance, Potochnik et al.'s definition looks very similar to the definition of "ideal intervention" that we find in manipulationist theories of causation, most notably, in James Woodward's version. Because some analysts have used Woodwardian concepts – ideal intervention, surgical intervention – in their actual analyses of scientific experimentation,[10] a brief clarification is in order.

Unlike Potochnik et al.'s definition, Woodward's definition of "ideal (experimental) intervention" is not primarily a characterization of scientific experimentation. Rather, his explication of an ideal intervention is in service of a theory of causation. The underlying idea is that causal claims (both in everyday life and in scientific practice) are best understood in terms of manipulation and control, that is, in terms of what we think is the best way in which causal claims can be established.

In the Woodwardian framework, the notion of *causation* is interpreted in terms of a manipulation on a certain variable for the purpose of determining whether the change of this variable causes another variable to change. More precisely, an intervention that fulfills the following conditions is a "surgical" intervention:

> [A]n intervention on *X* with respect to *Y* changes the value of *X* in such a way that if any change occurs in *Y*, it occurs only as a result of the change in the

[10] See Eronen (2020) for a recent example. I will return to the example in Section 6.

> value of X and not from some other source. This requires, among other things, that the intervention not be correlated with other causes of Y except for those causes of Y (if any) that are causally between the intervention and X or between X and Y, and that the intervention not affect Y via a route that fails to go through X. (Woodward 2003b, 14)[11]

Discussions about controlled experimentation, by contrast, follow the opposite route: *Experimentation* is interpreted in terms of a practice of inquiry that can generate claims about cause–effect relations. One then considers how experimental practice best achieves this purpose. The change of direction has an important implication. In interventionist theories of causality, the notion of intervention is formalized in deliberately non-anthropomorphic language. This is because there are processes that we would consider as causal but that cannot be conceived as "manipulations by humans" in any plausible way, such as gravitational attraction between celestial objects. Pragmatic accounts of experimentation, however, treat experimentation as human activity.[12] If the effect of an experimental intervention was not detected and (ultimately) perceived by an experimenter, one would not say that an experiment was carried out. Experimental outcomes must be such that it is possible for the experimenter to notice them directly or in form of a readable recording by a detector. Experimental control thus concerns not only the experimental setting in its environment, the experimental target, the intervention, and investigative tools but also the experimenter as intervening actor and recorder of events. The perfect registration or recording is targeted just at the changes thus produced; ideally, the experimenters register the effect of the intervention alone, not, say, an effect they hope to see, a side effect of the intervention, or an artifact generated by the recording device.

The ideal of perfectly controlled experiments, as spelled out by Potochnik et al., refers to a situation in which the experimenter has complete mastery and full grasp of the experimental setting. "Perfect control" means that all the factors that affect the experimental intervention are known and manipulable. This notion spells out what needs to be in place such that the experimenter can gain knowledge about the change of interest.

Another common way to think about perfectly controlled experimentation is along the lines of Boring's insight that all experimentation involves comparison to be informative. Here one acknowledges explicitly what is only implicit in the previous definition, namely that to understand what difference an intervention makes, we must compare it (explicitly, implicitly, counterfactually) with

[11] For a more detailed characterization of this idea, see Woodward (2003b, chapter 3).

[12] In a "natural experiment," nature would be the actor, so to speak.

a situation in which no intervention is made. This form of control has to do with warranting the causal role of the treatment or intervention. This concept of perfectly controlled experiment resonates with the Method of Difference from John Stuart Mill's *System of Logic* (Mill 1843).

In a perfectly controlled comparative trial, an experimental treatment or intervention is compared with a reference treatment (such as refraining from intervention) while everything else stays the same. Again, this is an abstract ideal, which expounds the conditions in which a causal claim is warranted. The formal exposition of its logic presupposes that all the factors that affect the experimental intervention are known and manipulable, as in the scenario discussed earlier.

Other accounts of "perfectly controlled" experiments aim further to clarify the epistemological issues while construing a notion of control that does not depend on the ability to identify or manipulate (hold fixed or exclude) literally all variables in an experimental setting. Francesco Guala has argued along these lines that the perfectly controlled experiment is comparative (like Mill's Method of Difference), and the comparison is between two *groups* of things or living beings, whereby the groups are situated in circumstances that vary with respect to only one factor – the intervention or treatment (Guala 2005, 65).

Comparing groups of things or beings instead of individuals is a pragmatic concession because this practice is a way to manage the inevitable variations among the group members. The idea here is that if the group is large enough, then its members could be considered alike. For every deviation in one direction, there is likely a deviation in the other direction, so they cancel each other out.[13] For each individual who dies from a severe urinary tract infection, there is another one who spontaneously recovers from it. For each individual whose chickenpox lasts two months instead of the typical two weeks, there is another who fully recovers within two days.

The RCT takes this idea and the pragmatic concessions one step further. Group assignments may not fully escape the problem of unequally distributed variations of variables across group members because they may reflect hidden experimenter preferences. In an RCT, the comparison is between two sets of trials, one consisting of a group of things (or living beings) that receive a treatment, the other consisting of a reference group not treated. In addition, assignment to these groups is randomized to counter possible selection effects, for instance certain preferences the experimenter may (unwittingly) follow in assigning the groups.[14] As Nancy Cartwright has shown, an ideal RCT

[13] For the history of this idea, see (Hacking 1990).

[14] Randomization is "the great *ceteris paribus* … of causal inference" (Cook and Campbell 1979, 5).

"clinches" a cause, as the ideal Millian experiment does. If the assumptions defining the ideal RCT are met, the conclusion that the intervention or treatment caused the differential trial outcome is deductively implied (Cartwright 2007, 2011).

2.3 Pragmatics of Experimental Control

The three notions of "perfectly controlled experiment" that I described in the previous subsection specify ideals. The first – the perfectly controlled intervention – encapsulates an ideal for scientific methodology. The notion is at the center of an abstract account of the conditions that must be in place for an experiment to generate empirical knowledge. Such an account provides an answer to the question of why a perfect intervention gives us empirical knowledge and of what kind of knowledge it generates – knowledge about the effects of changes the experimenter introduces in a target system.

The second and third notions of "perfectly controlled experiment" are explications of the notion of causation, understood in an interventionist framework. The fundamental idea underlying both is familiar from Mill's theory of causation: To establish a cause with certainty, we compare two situations that are identical. When one factor is changed in one situation, we can be sure that this change is the cause of subsequent changes that occur in that situation and not in the other.

How useful are these notions for the understanding of actual control practices in scientific inquiry? It is a commonplace in philosophy of science that epistemological ideals such as the ideal of a perfectly controlled experiment are never realized and indeed cannot be fully realized in scientific practice.[15] Recent philosophers of causation have acknowledged this point by characterizing actual experimental practice as "soft" (as opposed to surgical) intervention, whereby a soft intervention does not completely determine the value of the independent variable (Eberhardt and Scheines 2007). Actual interventions affect more than one variable – they are "fat-handed" (Woodward).[16]

Philosophers sometimes add that scientists strive to achieve epistemological ideals, whereby it depends on the concrete situation to what extent the ideal is approximated. But this is not a plausible claim. Scientists would rarely be able to specify the technicalities of epistemological arguments themselves, so they would "follow the ideal" without having it available or being able to explicate it. Also,

[15] Mill already made this point in his commentary on the methods of experimental inquiry. See also Cartwright's warning about the vanity of rigor in RCTs (Cartwright 2007).

[16] Fat-handed interventions are such that they affect "not just X and other variables lying on the route from I to X to Y, but also other variables that are not on this route and that affect Y" (Woodward 2008, 209).

the ideals are in principle impossible to instantiate. So, if scientists are not able to articulate, defend, and instantiate the ideal, it is hard to see how one could say that they seek to accomplish it in any meaningful sense.[17] Moreover, if one just considers scientists' practices as provisional or incomplete instantiations of epistemologically justified ideals, one is not doing justice to the things they *do* when they carry out research. One would certainly not simply call all experimental practice "uncontrolled" or "not sufficiently controlled" just because it falls short of the epistemological ideal.

The discussion in Section 2.2 is useful for a different reason, namely because it helps to pinpoint two distinct tasks connected to control: the management of the background against which an experimental intervention on a target system is going on, and the deliberate construction of an experimental arrangement for comparison, which resembles the experiment of interest in every way except for the intervention. Scientists commonly refer to the first task in terms of "controlling for" background factors. The second task is usually described in terms of "control experiment." Notably, making a control experiment also requires controlling for background factors, as both experimental situations have to be kept stable (except for the intervention) for the comparison to be informative.

In the remaining part of this Element, I examine actual solutions to control problems in experimentation, focusing on background factors and on strategies and practices to hold the background fixed or to maintain constancy. I draw attention to a whole other dimension to experimental control, namely the technical task of organizing the objects and tools. In an epistemological account, the notion of perfectly controlled intervention tells us what conditions need to be in place for causal inferences to be valid. In actual practice, control involves manipulating stuff. It involves deliberately introducing some change into an otherwise static situation and observing whether some other change occurs in that situation. The setting for the intervention must be actually held fixed. Moreover, to establish what factors need to be held fixed, second-order experimentation is often required.

3 Background Factors

3.1 Target System, Background, and Extraneous Factors

I have characterized an experiment as an intervention on a target system under study, whereby the experimenter registers or measures the change in the

[17] William Wimsatt even suggests that striving to follow the epistemological ideals may be harmful: "We are not LaPlacean demons, and any image of science that tells us how to behave as if we were still fails to give useful guidance for real scientist in the real world. In fact, it may suggest viewpoints and methods that are less than optimal for the dinky and error-prone equipment we possess" (Wimsatt 2007, 78).

behavior of the target system that the intervention brings about. I have also assumed that in order to determine the change or effect, the background in which the experimental intervention occurs must be held constant. If one is just concerned with defining causes and ideal interventions in the context of interventionist theories of causation, one can leave the background unspecified, as Woodward in fact does. Consider again his definition of causation. In the manipulationist framework, a cause is defined as "the notion of variable *X* such that, given other causal factors or background circumstances *that need not be explicitly described or represented*, changes in the value of *X* will result in changes in the value of some other variable *Y*" (Woodward 2003a, 91–92, emphasis added). In actual experimental inquiry, however, the background against which causation happens cannot be left unspecified.

Of course, there are many factors that one can set aside and safely ignore in an experiment. The number of penguins living in Antarctica is likely to be irrelevant for most experiments currently under way in the biomedical sciences. Extraneous factors need not be identified or explicitly described; indeed, it is impossible to specify them all. In contrast, the immediate surrounding of an experiment, such as a laboratory space, is relevant to experimental control. In controlled experimentation, background factors are targets of active management; they are explicitly considered and manipulated.

There are thus two sets of factors for experimental control: the set of background factors making up the situation in which the experiment goes on and "everything else," the factors deemed extraneous to the experiment.[18] Background factors and extraneous factors are complementary in that everything that is not deemed relevant to the experiment is an extraneous factor and, as such, need not be explicitly described. Nothing is background factor or extraneous factor simply by virtue of its internal makeup. Carving out the background from extraneous factors is relative to the point of view of the actor, the experimenter. It is the experimenter who treats certain factors as part of the background and to hold them fixed or considers them as (part of) a cause for the outcome of interest.

The distinction between background factors and target system is relational as well, and similarly dependent on experimenters' point of view. Notably, the distinctions may not map onto quotidian distinctions between experimenters, experimental objects, and instruments. What we would intuitively describe as the object of experimentation – an experimental animal, say, or

[18] This notion of "extraneous" is different from Potochnik et al.'s notion, to which I referred at the beginning of Section 2.2.

a human subject – might also have features that need to be considered part of the background. Consider, for instance, an experiment to examine whether the consumption of energy drinks causes insomnia in humans. To investigate the question, one might choose to study sleeping patterns in human beings who imbibe caffeinated soda. In this project, some features of the human subject – the age, size, diet, amount of exercise before the experiment – could be considered background factors that need to be appropriately managed for the study to yield informative results.

In the context of empirical investigation, experimenters need to attend to a specific kind of background factors, namely to what scientists often call "confounders." Confounders or confounding factors are the pesky things that get in the way of a successful intervention. They are causal factors that affect or get mixed up in the experimental process such that they distort, impede, or prevent the outcome of interest.

3.2 Formal Accounts of Confounders

One main context for discussions about confounders has been epidemiological research. Epidemiological studies typically are observational studies, whereby the co-occurrence of certain phenomena and events in populations is under scrutiny. Such phenomena and events could be exposure to toxic waste or contaminants in drinking water and prevalence of certain types of cancer or mortality, for example, or consumption of processed foods and cardiovascular diseases. The association between these phenomena in a population is studied through statistical analyses of collected data.

An influential epidemiological notion of confounding is based on potential outcome contrasts in comparisons of groups receiving similar treatments. As we saw in Section 2, the perfect RCT requires that the groups to be compared be equal in terms of the distribution of relevant variables across groups. If the groups are not comparable in terms of how these factors are being distributed, the result of the investigation is considered "confounded." According to Alfredo Morabia, the modern definition of confounding treats "non-comparability as the essence of confounding" (Morabia 2011, 299, but see also Fuller 2019).

In statistical terms, confounders are also frequently defined as variables that are associated with both the independent variable or "exposure" (e.g. consumption of processed foods) and the dependent variable or outcome (e.g. presence of heart disease). Confounders are also discussed in formal epistemology in relation to causal models. In this context, confounders are explicitly understood as causal factors, as variables affecting both the variable intervened upon and the dependent variable or effect. The confounder is sometimes labeled as "lurking variable," "third variable," or "common cause." This notion goes back to Hans Reichenbach, who formulated the common-cause principle in the context of his probabilistic theory of causation.[19] The common-cause principle posits that a correlation between two events is either due to a causal link or to a common cause, which brings about both.

Causal models offer a way to represent causal relations graphically through simple arrow diagrams.[20] The straightforward graphic tools allow graphic representation of a confounder as a variable from which two arrows point to two variables, the dependent and the independent variable, respectively. Other relations between variables can also be mapped easily, notably the "collider" and "mediator" relations between variables. A collider is a variable that is a common *effect* of both the independent and the dependent variable; it has thus two arrows pointed at it. A mediator is a variable that is impacted by the independent variable and, in turn, has an impact on the dependent variable: An arrow goes from the independent variable to it, and an arrow goes from it to the dependent variable.[21]

These graphic representations are a convenient tool to map more complicated causal nexus between numerous variables. It is also possible to formulate clear and straightforward rules about what to control and what not to control, even in complicated cases with many variables (Wunsch 2007). A researcher should control for confounders, those factors that affect both the independent and dependent variables, creating a spurious relation. The stock example to illustrate this is the strong correlation between drownings and ice cream sales. If we control for the season (the temperature) in our study, the connection will turn out to be spurious. A researcher should not control for colliders – for common effects of two variables, as controlling for a common effect of a treatment and an outcome creates a spurious association between the latter two. Consider, for instance, weight loss. It is a common effect of dieting and non-diet-related cancer. Dieting and this type of cancer are thus unrelated. If we run a study and control for weight loss, the two variables become associated: Within the group of individuals who lost weight, it is more likely that they have cancer if they are not on a diet.[22] And, a researcher should not control for mediators because it will change the measured connection between the independent and dependent variables.

Once all the relations between the variables in a study are mapped, one can conveniently read off the graph how the analysis should proceed. Formal

[19] Reichenbach 1956, see Illari and Russo 2014, 16–17.

[20] For an accessible account of causal models and their analysis, see Pearl and Mackenzie (2020).

[21] An example for a mediator would be "experience" in a study of the effect of the level of education on salary. The level of education has an impact on the level of experience an individual worker has, which, in turn, influences the individual's salary. The example is from Pearl and Mackenzie (2020, 275–276).

[22] The example is from Hernán et al. (2002).

accounts of confounders are especially useful for observational studies and computer-aided data analysis, where it is particularly challenging to distinguish mere associations from causal connections. Formal descriptions of confounders (and colliders and back-door variables) can be used to specify which associations between variables should be computed.

From a pragmatic perspective, however, the formal discussion of confounders is incomplete. The graphic mapping of causal relations, the formal characterization of confounders, mediators, and colliders leave open one of the biggest questions for actual experimental practice, namely how it is determined what the confounders, colliders, and mediators are in one's study.

The tools of formal causal analysis do not open a path to overcome the difficulties raised by the two scientists in the quote with which I began this Element – the challenge of designing appropriate controls. Judea Pearl simply notes that causal (path) analysis, including identifying confounders and biases, "requires scientific thinking" (Pearl and Mackenzie 2020, 84). Alas, the remaining part of this Element also cannot provide handy recipes for designing adequate controls, but it will flesh out what is involved in this process of "scientific thinking" – an alignment of knowledge, arguments, techniques, equipment, and skills.

3.3 Controlling the Background

I began this section with two distinctions, one between the target system and the background factors for an experiment, the other between target system-cum-background factors and extraneous factors deemed irrelevant for the experiment. These distinctions cut across quotidian distinctions between experimenter, experimental object, and instruments. Moreover, the difference between background and extraneous factors is a pragmatic distinction relative to the perspectives and interests of the experimenter. The distinction between target system and background is also pragmatic and context-dependent in a similar way.

I have been vague about the "factors" that make up background in which the experiment is happening and that may confound the experiment. If we try to give the notion of "factor" a more precise formulation, we run into an issue that I raised in the introduction to this Element, namely the tradeoff between formal epistemological analysis and pragmatic philosophical accounts. What are "background factors," metaphysically speaking? Are they phenomena, states, events, facts, or variables that can take on different values? I have also assumed that confounders are causal factors. But what is the relation or connection that holds between those factors and the causal nexus under study in the experiment? Should we characterize it via the concept of mechanisms, necessary and sufficient conditions, in terms of counterfactuals, agency, regularities, and probabilities?[23] Depending on how we conceive of the factors and the relata of a causal nexus, various additional conceptual puzzles arise. In an animal experiment involving hepatic ablation, for instance, an intervention is done on the liver of a live animal, for instance to destroy a small tumor by freezing, ethanol injection, or other means. Does the intervention bring about an event, one that causes certain other events in the animal? Or does it produce a state of affairs that causes another state of affairs? Or does it cause a variable to change? Conceptual puzzles of this kind are interesting and useful because they probe our understanding of "cause" and "causation." But, arguably, the intricacies of the construed cases that are typically devised to make progress on conceptual questions are of little import for the purpose of understanding the ways in which scientists grapple with problems of control, and I will therefore set them aside.

Pragmatically, background factors or control targets seem to fall into two categories. On the one hand, there are experimental conditions that need to be in place for an experiment to work, or to work well. Nineteenth-century physiologists could conduct their frog experiments only in temperatures above freezing; otherwise, the frogs would lapse into torpor and the effects could not be observed. Temperature is an experimental condition in this experiment – a background factor whose value needs to be within a certain range for the experiment to work. On the other hand, there are confounders, factors that interfere with the experimental process or prevent the effect from becoming manifest.[24] An optical aberration in an instrument, for instance, would be a confounder in this broad sense.

Strictly speaking, the distinction between conditions and confounders is unnecessary because the confounders present in an experiment could be reinterpreted as experimental conditions and vice versa. The lacteal vessels in animal bodies, as described by the Italian physician Gaspar Asellius in the seventeenth century, could only be observed during a certain time after the animal had eaten, for example. It depends on the way in which one describes the experiment whether the right time appears as a condition, or the wrong time appears as a confounder. Making the experiment at the right time is a condition for a successful outcome. But it would also be plausible to say that missing the right time slot interferes with the success of the outcome, in which case (incorrect) timing would be considered a confounder. On a pragmatic

[23] For an overview of the current discussion about the metaphysics of causation, see Gallow (2022). See also Beebee, Hitchcock, and Menzies (2009) and Fenton-Glynn (2021).

[24] See, for example, Overgaard (2004) for a discussion of confounding in consciousness studies along these lines.

understanding of "confounder" and "condition," the absence of the condition under which an experimental effect obtains is a confounding factor, as the experimental effect would be impeded or prevented. With this in mind, I will continue to use both the terms "condition" and "confounder" or "confounding factor."

Importantly, control targets are themselves targets of intervention in the sense that they are, at least in part, specified, produced, and shaped by the experimenters prior to and during the experimental intervention. Scientists must design and stabilize a setting, identify what the control targets are and how to deal with them, and run experiments accordingly. To do this, they need to draw on their prior understanding of the phenomena and processes that make up the experiment in its environment.

If confounders remain unrecognized, the experiment will likely yield incorrect conclusions. But even if they are recognized, it may not be easy to devise an appropriate process of controlling for them. This is a crucial point for the understanding of controlled experimentation. "Controlling for" background factors is importantly a technical task. "Controlling for" may require holding constant, detection, or removal. Recognizing the factors for which experimenters should control is only the first step in experimental design. It is one thing to realize that noise and vibrations interfere with an experiment. It is quite another thing to design a laboratory environment that keeps out such confounders. The history of scientific experimentation is full of episodes that illustrate how demanding the technical task can be. Nineteenth-century physiologists and physicists were actively involved in designing research institutes in which laboratories were built in remote parts or basements, away from student foot traffic and city noise.[25] In recent years, an entire industry has emerged that is devoted to solving such control tasks for scientists. Today's scientists can turn to specialized construction companies when they need "clean rooms" for their research. All-metal or all-plastic labs are built for research on the impacts of micro-plastics on materials and tissues or on radiation, respectively.

To sum up: This section has characterized an experiment as an intervention on a target system that goes on in an environment made up of (relevant) background factors situated in a world of extraneous factors that can be left unspecified. The distinctions between target system and background and between background and extraneous factors are relational and relative to the point of view of the experimenter. Background factors, control targets, can be described as conditions or confounders. "Controlling for" background factors is an epistemic as well as a technical task. Not only do control targets have to be

[25] See, e.g., Hoffmann (2001).

identified, but they have to be appropriately managed – detected, held constant, removed, as the case may be.

Finally, it is worth noting that everything I said in this section about controlling the background also applies to control experiments as they are characterized in Section 2. The comparison between an experimental intervention of interest and a control case is only informative if background factors are controlled across both experiments. In the next section, I refer to historical materials to flesh out these points.

4 Historical Perspectives on Controlled Experimentation

4.1 Investigating Spontaneous Generation

In Section 2, I took issue with the claim that scientists strive to achieve the ideal of perfect control in their experiments. I distinguished two key control tasks as they arise in experimentation: managing background factors and producing a warrant for a causal conclusion via comparative trials.

In this section, I further examine these tasks via the history of spontaneous generation research. The possibility of spontaneous generation of living beings was a long-standing problem that occupied researchers for centuries, stimulating much experimental activity. The history of theories about and attitudes to spontaneous generation is well studied because the religious and socio-cultural implications of ideas about the origin of life have been so profound. I can thus rely on (and direct the reader to) substantial historiography on theories of spontaneous generation. I approach this history from another angle, focusing on the control problems the researchers encountered as they experimented on spontaneous generation and examining how they dealt with those problems.[26] This section illustrates how control strategies are realized and what is involved in holding the background constant. I elucidate the technical tasks involved in the implementation of control strategies and the uncertainties and limitations of the technological solutions. I will become evident that in experimental control, technical–practical and conceptual aspects are closely intertwined. The success and failure of control measures depend on the alignment of theoretical ideas, arguments, practices, and tools. Moreover, the long-term perspective on control problems makes apparent that control targets are moving targets and objects of (second-order) experimentation.

[26] For ancient and premodern discussions, see Lehoux (2017). For later debates, see Ratcliff (2009), the classic account by Farley (1977), as well as Strick (2000). For a brief yet very informative overview, see Strick (2009). See also the collection of primary sources Strick has put together (Strick 2004). I will refer to more specific historiographical treatments throughout this section.

Investigations of spontaneous generation started in antiquity. The Italian Francesco Redi, the British John Turberville Needham and John Tyndall, the French naturalist Georges-Louis Leclerc, Comte de Buffon, the Italian Lazzaro Spallanzani, the French Louis Pasteur, and many other, lesser-known investigators weighed in – not least because larger religious, cultural, and metaphysical issues concerning the origin of life and disease and divine agency were at stake.

In popular science writing and science education literature (and on the internet), both Redi's and Pasteur's experiments are cited as outstanding examples of controlled experimentation.[27] Redi's experiments on allegedly spontaneous appearance of maggots from dead matter, in which he compared open and covered jars of putrefying meat, are frequently described as the first control experiments. Pasteur's instruments, the iconic swan-necked flasks, are presented as emblematic of modern science because they allowed the experimenter to manipulate and reign in sub-visible germs and thus settle the debates about spontaneous generation.

Of course, the actual experiments were much more complicated than the popular and science education literature suggests. Redi's experiments were not the first control experiments. Neither his nor Pasteur's experiments were in fact decisive. The reason why Redi's experiments on spontaneous generation have often been called "the first control experiments" is that he used comparative designs.[28] In his investigations of the generation of life from dead materials, first published in 1688, he compared samples of organic materials – "a snake, some fish, some eels of the Arno, and a slice of milk-fed veal in four large, wide-mouthed flasks" (Redi 1909, 33). One set of flasks was open, another "well closed and sealed" (Redi 1909, 33). The open vessels were soon teeming with maggots. In the sealed flasks, no maggots appeared, although Redi had also frequently observed flies in the vicinity of these vessels. He concluded that the maggots came from fly eggs and were not spontaneously generated in the container.[29]

Redi explicitly highlighted that he had made comparative trials, several of them, for the purpose of "confirmation" (Redi 1909, 33). Nevertheless, Redi also made clear that he himself did not consider the trials decisive. He noted: "Not content with these experiments, I tried many others at different seasons, using different vessels. In order to leave nothing undone, I even had pieces of meat put under ground, but though remaining buried for weeks, they never bred worms, as was always the case when flies bad been allowed to light on the meat" (Redi 1909, 34).

[27] James Conant used spontaneous generation research as an illustration of biological experimentation and control in his introduction to scientific method *Science and Common Sense*, originally published in 1951. But as we will see at the end of this section, his conclusion differs from mine.

[28] In the popular and science education literature, this comparative design is often identified as an *avant-la-lettre* instance of Mill's Method of Difference. For a recent example, see Allchin (2020).

[29] See Parke (2014) and Bertoloni Meli (2009) for more details of the project and historical context.

In this, as well as in other projects, Redi also made a point about the importance of repeating experiments, as contingent events might impede individual trials.[30]

The experiments with flies and maggots were narrow in scope.[31] They did not end the debates about spontaneous generation. Subsequent researchers all used comparative experimental designs and repeated their experiments or compared groups of things. They made comparative trials both to single out the cause that brought about the life developing in their flasks and jars and to examine how particular background factors impacted their trial designs. But they had very different understandings of what exactly had to be manipulated, how the control case had to be constructed, and thus what exactly it meant to control for background factors in their experiments.

In the mid-eighteenth century, John T. Needham investigated spontaneous generation both by himself and together with Comte de Buffon.[32] Needham claimed that he could demonstrate the spontaneous generation of living matter in infusions. He had a theory about how spontaneous generation would come about; he assumed that inanimate "organic molecules" existed and that the vegetative power residing in those organized molecules could generate life. Living beings could and would therefore develop in a vessel containing inanimate organic matter even if it was hermetically sealed and no seeds, eggs, or germs could enter from outside.

Unlike Redi, Needham dealt with invisible things, which raised the stakes for good experimental practice. Flies, and even their eggs, are visible with the naked eye or with a lens, but Needham had to keep his flasks free from invisible eggs or seeds floating in the air or in the liquid contained in the flask. He experimented with "Mutton-Gravy hot from the Fire," which he put in a vial "clos'd up with a Cork so well masticated, that my Precautions amounted to as much as if I had sealed my Phial hermetically." Sealing the flask and heating the fluid and the sealed vial would destroy any life present in the flask and prevent contamination, so he assumed. Needham told his readers that he had "neglected no Precaution, even as far as to heat violently in hot Allies the Body of the Phial; that if any thing existed, even in that little Portion of Air which filled up the Neck, it might be destroy'd, and lose its productive Faculty" (Needham 1748, 637–638). Regardless of all the precautions Needham took to prepare the apparatus and the organic

[30] For a more detailed discussion of the role of repetitions in early modern experimentation, see Schickore (2017, especially chapters 2 and 3).

[31] In the case of gall insects, Redi came to a different conclusion about their origin, allowing that they were generated by the trees, that is, through heterogenesis. The investigation of the origin of gall wasps was an observational, not an experimental, study. For a detailed discussion of the two projects, see Parke (2014). See also Strick (2009).

[32] For a more detailed account, see Sloan (1992).

materials, the outcome was always the same: The infusion would be teeming with life. These living things must appear spontaneously.

The priest and naturalist Lazzaro Spallanzani famously sought to show, against Needham, that spontaneous generation did not happen in such infusions. His experimental reports presented countless experiments, too many to discuss them all here.[33] Like Redi and Needham, Spallanzani described his various operations and precautions. He did not use the term "control" in his report, but like Redi and Needham, he described comparative trials – control experiments – as evidence for causal claims. At the same time, he questioned the demonstrative power of Needham's comparative trials. His work exemplifies one of the central points of this Element, namely that the management of background factors is the epistemologically fundamental feature of controlled experimentation.

Spallanzani opened his report with Needham's experimental demonstration:

> We are told they [animalcules] must either come from specific seeds, or be produced by the vegetative power; that the first cannot take place, because they are found in close vessels subjected to the action of heat, equally as in open vessels, whereas the included germs, if there were any, ought not to survive. Therefore, they must originate from the vegetative power alone. (Spallanzani 1803, 2–3)

Spallanzani took issue with the design of this experiment. To put it in the terms introduced in previous sections, he argued that Needham had not properly controlled for background factors. In particular, Spallanzani doubted that heating the vial like Needham had would kill all living matter present in the fluid or in the little portion of air left in the flask.

Spallanzani engaged in an extensive project examining the resistance to heat of animalcules, eggs, and seeds. The experiments to check on Needham's experimental design became a research program in itself. Different kinds of infusions were boiled for extended periods (up to several hours). Microscopic life would flourish, nonetheless. In direct contradiction to Needham's claims, Spallanzani found that after a shorter period of heating fewer infusoria were generated. He found that some microscopic things (seeds, in particular) could withstand extremely high heat, and "superior" animalcules, by contrast, are killed by it. Spallanzani also used flasks that were melted shut instead of stopped with a cork. It was only when the infusions were exposed to prolonged heat *and* the flasks were sealed by melting their necks shut that no, or few, animalcules would appear in the infusions. Any "superior" animals appearing in solutions previously boiled must get into the solution from somewhere else – from the residual air in the flask, as Spallanzani surmised.

[33] See Prescott (1930) for a detailed reconstruction of Spallanzani's multilayered project.

Because watery infusions could not be boiled above 100 °C (212 °F), Spallanzani also subjected vegetable seeds to other forms of heat. For instance, different kinds of seeds were "slowly heated in a coffee roaster until they became pretty well roasted." They generated animalcula even after they were "burnt and ground the same as we burn and grind coffee" (Spallanzani 1803, 11). The vegetable seeds were "exposed to the greatest heat that can be excited by common fires, or fire augmented by art. Burning coals, and the flame of the blow pipe, were the two agents exercising their power on them" (Spallanzani 1803, 12). The animalcules did not come from the water, Spallanzani added. He had repeated the trials and compared the infusions with pure water (with a control, in modern terms), showing that "not one was seen in the water" (Spallanzani 1803, 13).

The extensive work comprised many more experiments on various features of microscopic life, such as resistance to cold and desiccation. But were they better controlled than Needham's or Redi's? Arguably, this is an intractable question. Redi experimented with visible things, with rotting meat (snake, fish, veal). He used very simple tools – wide-mouthed jars, paper, gauze, and twine, which were easy to manipulate. He could thus easily track target systems and background factors by observation. Potential confounders – the egg-laying flies – were effectively excluded from the setting in one set of trials. The comparison between the trials was as straightforward as the instruments, and the management of background factors was simple.

Spallanzani's project, by contrast, yielded more complex answers to more intricate questions about spontaneous generation (and several other issues) than previous endeavors had. Spallanzani's multiple experiments relied on elaborate theoretical arguments, for instance concerning the organization of organic matter and the classification of animalcules into higher and lower with different properties. His experiments required more complicated technology than previous experiments, such as vessels with very thin necks, the skills to close them by melting those necks, blowpipes that could generate high temperatures, and precise thermometers and pendula to measure temperature and time.[34] Intuitively, we would say that Spallanzani's experiments were at least better controlled than Needham's because he developed more effective ways to close the flasks and heat up the infusions. But, in hindsight, it is obvious that Spallanzani's evidence and arguments also depended on several additional, tacit assumptions about the nature and properties of animalcules, organic matter and its organization, the experimental environment, and the working of the tools he used to investigate those things. Both these assumptions and the initial

[34] Notably, Spallanzani's microscope was technically inferior compared to the instrument Needham and Buffon were using (Sloan 1992).

findings from his experiments had implications for the design of his subsequent experiments on spontaneous generation, concerning the length of the boiling process, the manner of sealing, and the preparation of the seeds he used in his trials, among other things. It was not as evident as in Redi's case that his technical arrangements were effectively doing what they were supposed to do; their effectiveness could only be inferred given various additional assumptions about the working of the equipment, the target system, and the experimental environment.

Spallanzani's experiments were also not deemed entirely conclusive. The debates continued. In 1836, a couple of decades before Pasteur experimented with the swan-necked flasks, the Berlin chemist Franz Schulze, assistant to the then well-known chemist Eilhard Mitcherlich, raised the question of how life *could* possibly appear in containers that had been boiled vigorously to sterilize them. In such a container, he reckoned, there would be no air for the budding life to breathe.[35] For him, the control task changed once more, as new background factors came into view with that consideration. Air had to be admitted to the infusion, but it had to be free from biotic matter. In Schulze's words, "first, one would have to be sure at the beginning of the trial that no animals or seeds capable of development were present in the infusion and second, that the incoming air did not contain any of that" (Schulze 1836, 487). Schulze was, as Pasteur himself later pointed out, noncommittal about the kind of matter that might be in the air; he just wanted to exclude any thing "capable of development." But, regardless of what these things were, how could one determine their presence, given that they were invisible?

Schulze did not attempt to do this; he just tried to safeguard his experiment. To purify air and cleanse it from whatever "animals or seeds" may float in it, Schulze employed the latest available chemical technology. He introduced a tool that, he assumed, could do the job. This was a contraption with two of Justus Liebig's *Kaliapparaten* on both sides of a glass vessel filled with distilled water and boiled vigorously.[36] One *Kaliapparat* was filled with sulfuric acid, the other with caustic potash solution. The contraption was placed in the warm sunlight. Several times a day, Schulze would suck air by mouth (!) through the device with the caustic potash solution, thus ensuring (he hoped) that all living matter that might be floating in the air would be destroyed as it passed through

[35] Schulze did not refer to Spallanzani.

[36] A *Kaliapparat* consists of five glass bulbs, which are connected by thin glass tubes and arranged to form a triangle. When an organic substance is burned, the carbon in it forms a gas, which passes through the bulbs, which are filled with potassium hydroxide solution. The product of its reaction with the gas can be trapped and from it the amount of carbon in the original substance can be calculated. For a description of this convenient tool, which had originally been developed for organic analysis, see Liebig (1831).

the sulfuric acid. He could not visually check whether this measure was successful; he had reason to believe it was, based on what he knew the tool could do and what he knew about the effects of caustic potash solution, a common cleansing agent, on biotic matter.

Like everyone else, Schulze then made a comparative trial with his controlled setup, using an open vessel with no air filters as control case. The open vessel was soon teeming with various life forms, which he identified as vibrions, monads, and bigger infusoria. The other vessel did not show any trace of life, not even after more than two months. Then, after Schulze opened it, he found that infusoria, mold, and confervae appeared rapidly.

Pasteur's flasks were yet another technical solution to the same problem that Schulze faced: Air needed to get into the flasks, but just air, no biotic matter. Pasteur found a different way to manipulate what he assumed might be biotic matter getting into the flask. While Schulze had tried to destroy it, the long, curved neck of Pasteur's flask would trap it.

Theoretical assumptions suggested that the curved neck would trap the invisble biotic matter. Second-order experiments ascertained the effectiveness of the arrangement. Pasteur made experiments in which he broke the neck of the flask and sealed it again. He reckoned that in this intervention, the air would rush into the flask, thereby carrying the germs in the neck into the liquid, and infusoria would appear. He made this experiment, not once, but several times in different environments, and it worked – at least more often than not, and better in closed rooms that were known to contain relatively many germs, as opposed to mountain tops, where the air was thought to be cleaner.

What if microscopic life forms *had* appeared in Schulze's experiment, would that finding have demonstrated spontaneous generation? Or just the inadequacy of his setup for the purpose of screening off unknown causal factors obstructing the experiment? The problem did not emerge for Schulze (at least he did not report anything like it), but Pasteur faced such a situation in his debate with the naturalist Félix Pouchet. Pasteur's adversary demonstrated the generation of microbial life in a setting with air presumed to be free of biotic matter and boiled hay infusions in a mercury trough. Pasteur took the contradicting experimental evidence seriously and eventually pointed to a flaw in Pouchet's experimental design.

On the assumption that life could not be generated spontaneously, there must have been some other factors producing the life forms Pouchet had observed. As the contamination could not have come from the air or the sterile infusion (so Pasteur assumed), it must have come from the mercury trough, specifically from the atmospheric dust gathered on the surface of the trough. Notably, Pasteur did not just rely on these inferences but carried out second-order experiments to demonstrate the proper working of the original experimental setting. He showed that it was possible to generate life from tiny mercury balls.[37]

This was not the end of the debate. Researchers in Britain and elsewhere continued to investigate questions related to spontaneous generation. They were embroiled in debates and experiments about background factors and their possible roles for the generation of life that were quite similar to the exchanges between Pasteur and Pouchet as well as the issues at stake for Needham and Spallanzani. They found their own solutions to the control problems everyone faced, but none of their solutions were completely perfect.[38]

John Tyndall, who agreed with Pasteur that spontaneous generation from abiotic matter did not exist, built his own device to demonstrate this after he had become involved in a debate with the physiologist Henry Charlton Bastian. Bastian claimed to have experimental evidence in favor of spontaneous generation. He showed that living organisms developed in infusions of boiled turnip and cheese after the infusions were boiled for several minutes and hermetically sealed. During the ensuing debates, several investigators discussed various possible sources of contamination in Bastian's experiments, others engaged in extensive projects to establish the existence of the contaminating matter experimentally.

Several of these researchers explicitly conceded that circumstances and experimental designs were never completely ideal. They tried to address the problem by repeating trials multiple times, varying conditions and target systems, and tweaking the design. Nevertheless, experiments could not be expected to be decisive. In 1874, the doctor William Roberts described a total of ninety trials with infusions sterilized by heat, using substances ranging from milk, blood, and urine to orange juice and turnip tissue. Just sixty-seven showed no germination. For Roberts, this was to be expected, as:

> the ideal conditions of the experiments could not in any case be carried out with absolute stringency. Some risk of extraneous infection was always encountered in conveying the materials of the experiments into the sterilized bulbs and tubes. The results obtained are therefore not altogether uniform; but

[37] According to Gerald Geison's account of the dispute (1995, chapter 5), Pasteur emerged as the "winner" because he had strong political allies, not because he had the better methodology. True, Pouchet and indeed Schulze and Spallanzani availed themselves of similar experimental strategies, none of which were decisive. The conclusions these researchers drew were underdetermined by the experimental outcomes, and to explain why certain experimental results were broadly accepted while others were not, one will need to resort to additional considerations. Notably, other historians have doubted that Pasteur was indeed a "winner" to the extent that Geison claimed (see Strick 2000, Raynaud 2015, chapter 2), thus reducing that need. But it is not my concern here to resolve these historiographical disputes; rather, I wish to illuminate the complexity and limitations of control measures.

[38] See, for the following, Strick (2000).

> as this was in accordance with the expectation of the experiments, it adds to, rather than detracts from, their validity. (Roberts 1874, 471)

Roberts did find, on a few occasions, that germination happened in sterilized infusions after a very long period (months, in one case). In these instances, the organisms that appeared were not bacteria but fungoid. Roberts thus ended his report on a cautious note, conceding that these few experiments supported the existence of abiogenesis in some cases, but that the overwhelming majority of instances in which life was generated in test bulbs were due to organic materials imported into the bulb either by air or water.

The versatile physicist, naturalist, and geologist John Tyndall continued along these lines, constructing a device that was supposed to keep biotic matter out of the test tubes more effectively than Roberts' design did. His solution was to create a dust-free box, which was coated on the inside with glycerin and thus could trap dust particles. It had windows, so one could send a beam of light through it and visually check on the amount of dust in the air of the chamber (Strick 2000, 173).[39] Open test tubes with boiled infusions remained unchanged in the chamber.

In 1877, however, Tyndall himself announced that some of his recent experiments carried out in the dust-free chamber did show growth of living organisms in infusions. It was only after further experimentation, informed and inspired by the work of German biologist Ferdinand Cohn, that Tyndall managed to fix his experiments such that microbial growth was prevented.

Cohn, on his part, also conducted numerous experiments on the organic matter that the other researchers were struggling to understand. This was in the context of his broader work on the classification of microorganism and the study of their development, physiological makeup, and action. He and his coworkers made extensive experiments to investigate the heat-resistance of bacteria, noting that other researchers had produced "uncertain and contradictory" results (Cohn 1872, 217). Studying pea infusions at different temperatures, they found that putrefaction reliably occurred within a few days if the concoction was heated to less than 60 °C and did not occur at temperatures higher than

[39] The demonstration of dust in the air by making it visible with a beam of light had been one of the ways in which Pasteur tried to convince his audience that spontaneous generation did not exist. Roberts was rather dismissive of this effort, commenting: "The ingenious attempts of Pasteur and others to demonstrate germs in the air are manifestly illusory. Like them I have repeatedly collected air-dust and found abundance of molecules, circles, spheres, and particles of various kinds under the microscope; but these could not be identified as true spores, nor distinguished from particles of inert dust. Indeed the objects sought after are so minute and so wanting in characteristic forms, that such a search, with our present instruments, appears well-nigh hopeless. But although an obscurity hangs over the precise nature of these particles, the reality of their existence is not doubtful" (Roberts 1874, 472).

80 °C. To explain the mixed results at temperatures in between they examined possible confounders. Only the bulbous part of the flask was immersed in the boiling water, not the neck, so that the bacteria could survive in the cooler part, but a change of the experimental design did not bring more uniformity in the results. The researchers then suspected that solid and dry materials might shield the bacteria from the heat, as they were "notoriously bad heat conductors." Further investigations were thus done with an "artificial," that is, a "normal nutrient solution" (Cohn 1872, 118). Trials with bacteria in this solution in little flasks whose necks were closed by melting showed "without exception" that heating for an hour at 60 °C was sufficient to kill the bacteria. At this point, Cohn explicitly stated that control experiments had been carried out, adding: "As parallel and control experiments, two test tubes were always filled with the same bacteria fluid and not boiled; one of them melted shut, the other left open; both always showed rich multiplication of bacteria; which clearly demonstrated their and their comrades' ability to live" (Cohn 1872, 219).

Cohn knew of Bastian's work on hay infusions with turnip and cheese and launched a series of experiments on heat resistance in bacteria. Because it seemed most likely that germs could survive the heat inside the solid lump of cheese than in the boiled plant tissue, he started with an investigation of the bacteria involved in cheese making and identified "ferment organisms" in rennet, which generated spores as part of their life cycle. Those spores, he surmised, could survive the heat enclosed in the cheese lump and would then develop in the infusion, nourished by the turnip decoction (Cohn 1872, 195).

I cannot do justice to all the participants and twists and turns in the research on spontaneous generation, but the relevant points should now be clear: Virtually all researchers made control experiments, that is, they compared their sealed or insulated test tubes to test tubes exposed to the open air – in most cases to demonstrate that all kinds of life forms appeared in the latter, none emerged in the former. But the more momentous efforts concerned the organization and management of background factors. Over time, and often collectively, researchers worked out what they deemed the most appropriate designs for research on spontaneous generation. To do so, they studied different types of "germs" (biotic matter capable of producing microbial life) involved in making an infusion turbid, their possible origins in air and water, and their resistance to adverse conditions. Based on their assumptions about the features of this biotic matter, they tried to find the best ways to sterilize an infusion (i.e. to inactivate the biotic matter), and the best techniques to shield the containers from it. The researchers made numerous trials on infusions with diverse organic materials, ranging from body fluids and foodstuffs to plant tissues; they repeated trials, or made their trials on groups of flasks, to take care of contingent factors; and they designed and built increasingly elaborate devices to be able to insulate fluid and deactivate biotic matter. Many researchers carried out second-order experiments on the setting of their experiments.

Most researchers explicitly pointed out that the results they had obtained were not decisive, and they referred to less-than-ideal solutions to control problems as a reason. Notably, several of them, including Pasteur, Roberts, and Cohn, described extensively in their reports how they had tweaked and modified their tools to sterilize their flasks and to prevent biotic materials from entering the infusions. Today, these details are usually not part of the published research articles but become visible only to those who are part of a research group or interact directly with its members (see Section 6).

4.2 Investigating Abiogenesis

In the late nineteenth century, skepticism about spontaneous generation was common. In the 1950s, the tide turned when abiogenesis became a topic of chemical experimentation.[40] It is instructive to make a comparison between the control tasks arising from nineteenth-century experiments on spontaneous generation and from the experiments on the origin of life that the two chemists Harold Urey and Stanley Miller carried out in the mid-twentieth century.[41] Of course, the theoretical foundations of, and motivations for, these experiments were very different from the eighteenth- and nineteenth-century predecessors. Most importantly, Urey and Miller were convinced that abiogenesis did in fact happen, but for them, it was a process in the early history of the earth, a synthesis of organic molecules – amino acids – that had nothing to do with the emergence of organized life from abiotic matter as envisaged, or scorned, by eighteenth- and nineteenth-century scientists. Nevertheless, the control strategies reported in the publications on abiogenesis evidence familiar concerns.

Urey and Miller's experimental idea was to try to produce basic organic compounds from simple reagents, using an electric discharge as a trigger in their formation. The apparatus is supposed to be a mini model of the primordial earth. The main part of the experiment is a flask filled with water vapor, which simulates evaporation from the ocean, and a mixture of methane, ammonia, and hydrogen gases. This mixture was sparked with electric discharges for several days to simulate lightning discharge. The water became brownish yellow. Chromatographic analysis showed that amino acids had been formed.

[40] Again, I am simplifying the narrative. Alexander Oparin's book on the origin of life, which appeared in English translation in 1938, was an important milestone in the debate, but it was largely a theoretical proposal about the chemical evolution of life (Oparin 1938, see Strick 2009).

[41] See, among others, Urey (1952), Miller (1953), Hough and Rogers (1956), and Miller and Urey (1959); for overviews, see Lazcano and Miller (1996) and Lazcano and Bada (2003).

In the subsequent experiments, the conditions were slightly changed; higher pressure was used, and the means of discharge were varied from electric sparks to silent discharge.

This experiment illustrates the alignment of theoretical arguments, techniques, equipment, and skills that characterized other spontaneous generation experiments and that is so crucial for controlled experimentation. The creation of the "primordial atmosphere" in the flask is informed by chemico-physical theories about its likely composition, made possible by technical arrangements, and infused with pragmatic considerations. For instance, equal amounts of methane and ammonia were used so that "appreciable quantities of carbon and nitrogen would react in the spark." Miller added that the uncertainty about the initial composition of earth's atmosphere was such that any other choice would be "just as arbitrary" (Miller 1955, 2353).

As in the older, nineteenth-century experiments, the main technical tasks are sterilization and insulation of the content of the apparatus, which were realized as the modern equipment demanded, and as well as it permitted. Comparative trials – "blank runs with the same gases but no spark" – addressed the possibility that the amino acids could have been produced by microorganisms from the gases, as the amount of amino acids produced was negligible (Miller 1955, 2359). To ensure that no microorganisms were involved in the production of amino acids from the compounds produced by the discharge, extensive cleaning techniques were used, ranging from cleaning, checking for leaks heating the apparatus to placing it in an autoclave for eighteen hours,[42] after which the seal was again checked for leaks. After these extensive preparation procedures, the same amount of amino acids was produced when the experiment was run. "For these reasons," Miller noted, "it is stated with confidence that the organic compounds in this system were synthesized without the aid of microorganisms" (Miller 1955, 2359).

Urey and Miller's experiments were intensely discussed, repeated, and varied. From the perspective of experimental control, a recent set of experiments by Joaquin Criado-Reyes and coworkers (Criado-Reyes et al. 2021) is particularly striking. This group has examined the apparatus used in the Urey–Miller experiments and has demonstrated that the inner surfaces of the borosilicate flasks leak a slight amount of silica during the experiment. The researchers do so by comparing amino acid production in borosilicate flasks, Teflon flasks, and Teflon flasks containing pieces of borosilicate submerged in water. The brown liquid obtained in the Teflon flask with submerged borosilicate pieces contained

[42] An autoclave is a pressurized steam sterilizer used for killing bacteria, viruses, and fungi. It is used in industrial and clinical contexts.

more organic compounds than in Teflon flasks, and even more organic compounds were obtained in borosilicate flasks. Notably, the investigators do not interpret the borosilicate as contamination of the experiment, and thus due to lack of control of background factors. Rather, they conclude that silicate-rich rocky surfaces played a significant role in the production of the first organic compounds and that Urey–Miller's initial experiments had thus modeled the conditions of the primordial earth more accurately than previously assumed.

4.3 The Complexity of Control Tasks

This is only a cursory account of a complicated history involving many other events and occurrences and a host of other protagonists. I have reviewed this history here primarily to showcase some constants, continuities, transformations, and contingencies in the management of control problems in experimentation, as well as the increasing complexity of the control tasks involved.

All researchers reported multiple repetitions of their trials – with six flasks, with four flasks, sometimes with dozens of samples – in acknowledgement that nature does not always behave uniformly. Repeating trials, or using large samples, is one of the most basic safeguards against unknown, unspecified, haphazard events impacting the experimental process.

Virtually all researchers reported comparative trials – the comparison of an experimental case with a control case – to bolster a causal claim. However, they routinely acknowledged that comparative trials could not demonstrate causes with certainty. On occasion, they questioned whether a particular comparative trial design was at all suitable for demonstrating what it was supposed to demonstrate because some background conditions had not been fully accounted for. That concern powered much of Spallanzani's research project.

Referring to Redi's work, James Conant distinguished two aspects of experimental control in biology, the control of variables and the comparative trial, the latter being "the essence of the control experiment in biology" (Conant 1961, 235). In my analysis, the former is the more fundamental. The conceptualization, organization, and active management of background factors are requisite conditions for both the comparative trial and the repetition of trials. This endeavor has technical-practical and conceptual aspects; over time, it has involved increasingly more complex apparatuses, as well as assumptions about, and practical explorations of, how exactly certain background factors might impact the experimental process.

The endeavor involves what past experimenters often called "variation of circumstances," the systematic exploration of features of the setting to figure out how they might affect the experiment. To ascertain this, experimenters also made comparative trials on these features. Several of the spontaneous generation researchers engaged in extensive projects of this sort. This kind of second-order experimentation is a key component of *making* – devising, constructing, and carrying out – controlled experiments.

5 Control Strategies in Longue Durée

Experimental control is often considered as a modern phenomenon. Indeed, the *terms* "experimental control," "control experiment," and their cognates become frequent only during the latter part of the nineteenth century. But if we define experimentation *as* controlled intervention, then control begins when experimentation begins; the history of controlled experimentation begins when the first experiments were made.

Section 4 illustrated more specific control strategies. As we have seen, they have different epistemic functions within experimental practice. The comparative trial or comparison with a control is a way of establishing causes for effects. The repetition of trials is a way of dealing with unknown, contingent circumstances. The active organization of background factors enables the experimenter to recognize the changes induced by the experimental intervention.

The comparison between the effects of an intervention in a particular situation and the same situation without the intervention has been described as an "almost instinctive" way of establishing cause–effect relations (Mackie 1980, 71). Of course, the more distant the past, the more difficult it is to ascertain what strategies inquirers actually implemented when they experimented and whether they experimented at all. Present-day analysts of science must often resort to explicit descriptions of strategies in historical sources.[43]

The first textual traces of control measures in experimentation can be found in antiquity. Given that the comparison between the effects of an intervention in a particular situation and the same situation without the intervention is such a deep-seated way of establishing cause–effect relations, it should not come as a surprise that examples of this practice are described in ancient texts. Those scholars who have looked for "the first" controlled experiment (*avant la lettre*) have identified one in the Old Testament, the Book of Daniel, Book I. Servants on a vegetarian diet are compared with children who eat "the king's meat": "And at the end of ten days their countenances appeared fairer and fatter in

[43] The history of discourse about control experiments – the story of how and when experimenters highlighted this aspect, and what implications they tied to it – is a topic of interest in itself. That history is a part of the history of philosophy of science. As Section 4 indicates, it is also a long history.

flesh than all the children which did eat the portion of the king's meat" (Daniel 1:5–16).[44]

A passage by Athenaeus (AD 200) describes how some convicted criminals had been thrown among the asps and survived. It turned out that they had been given lemons prior to their punishment. The next day a piece of lemon was given to one convict, but not to another. The one who ate the lemon survived the bites, the other died instantly. In the pseudo-Galenic treatise on theriac, a trial is described with a similar design, whereby two birds would be poisoned and only one would be given an antidote (Leigh 2013). The trial is a test for the efficacy of medicines: If both animals survived, the tested antidote was recognized to be ineffectual. That experiment was again reported in the Middle Ages, notably by Bernard Gordon (McVaugh 2009). And as we have seen in the last section, the spontaneous generation researchers often pointed out that they had made comparative trials.

These experiments function as confirmations of causal inferences. If anything is remarkable about them, it is the fact that the earliest accounts of such experiments are usually from medical texts or contexts. Here I cannot offer a sustained historical argument for the claim that methodologies of control experiments originated in medical contexts. But it is a plausible claim, given that it is literally vitally important – and of course often also commercially important – to figure out the efficacy of certain drugs and treatments and that the reputation of a practitioner depended on the success of the treatments.[45]

Arguably, repeating trials, the implicit acknowledgement that various unknown, accidental, hard-to-control factors might impinge on an experiment, can also be considered as an almost instinctive way of ascertaining empirical knowledge. The ancient physician and anatomist Galen emphasized the importance of repetitions in the context of clinical observation because he was well aware of the fact that what one has seen only once in a patient may not be a regular occurrence and therefore unworthy of belief and acceptance. He mobilized Aristotle's concept of experience, according to which sensory perceptions give rise to memory, repeated memories of the same thing give rise to one single experience, and experience is the starting point of art and

[44] See Stigler (1974). This example is also quoted on the website of the Institute for Creation Research as a model for sound experimental design (Treece 1990). See also Pearl and Mackenzie (2020).

[45] There are non-medical examples for comparative trials in ancient texts. One is the legend of Pythagoras, who, as the story goes, discovered that most combinations of blacksmiths' hammers generate a harmonious sound when striking anvils at the same time, while others did not. Pythagoras discovered that harmonious sounds were produced by those hammers whose masses were simple ratios of each other; other hammers would make a disagreeable noise when struck simultaneously. Notably, Ptolemy later criticized the Pythagorean experiment because, to Ptolemy, it lacked control (Zhmud 2012, 307).

science (*Posterior Analytics* II, 19). Galen also drew attention to the fact that medicaments work sometimes, but not all the time. In clinical medicine, at least, one single drug test might not produce reliable results, because "some things are frequent and some are rare" (Galen 1944). The test must be repeated several times, and even then, it may not tell us what the case is usually.[46]

The Islamic philosopher and physicist Ibn Sīnā (Avicenna) expressed a similar idea in his proposal for rules of drug testing, albeit with a positive spin. He noted: "The effect of the drug should be the same in all cases or, at least, in most. If that is not the case, the effect is then accidental, because things that occur naturally are always or mostly consistent."[47] Medicine, especially the practically, socially, and economically significant context of successful drug testing, is an important ancient source of ideas and concerns about isolated events and repeated experiences. According to these ancient scholars, our memory is not always reliable. Moreover, things, including living beings, sometimes behave in unusual ways. Therefore, observations and (drug) trials should always be repeated several times.

In the mid-seventeenth century, the experimental philosopher and member of the Royal Society Robert Boyle wrote two essays on "unsucceeding" experiments, in which he described "the Contingencies to which Experiments are obnoxious upon the account of Circumstances, which either are constantly unobvious, or at least are scarce discernable till the Tryal be past" (Boyle 1669, 75). Boyle, who participated in or witnessed many experiments, knew well that experimental interventions can be obstructed in various ways, and he attempted to give his readers an idea of the scope of the problem.[48] He provided a list of obstacles for successful experimentation. Problems could arise because some experimenters may have made "as well use of their Imagination as of their Eyes" (Boyle 1669, 82), or because of the "unskilfulness of the Tryers of the Experiments" (Boyle 1669, 44). Experiments could be unsuccessful due to "unsuspected difference of the Materials imploy'd about them" such as the impurity of chemicals (Boyle 1669, 60). Mineralists and metallurgists searching for metal veins in the "bowels of the Earth" (Boyle 1669, 50) had to contend with divining rods that did not always work reliably, gardeners and anatomists

[46] These considerations are part of an elaborate discussion of empiricism and dogmatism in medicine. Galen put forward this point in the middle of his attempt to demonstrate that medical practice is not just logos but also experience. A large part of the text is a rebuttal of the sorites argument according to which it is impossible to clarify the notion of seeing something "very many times" (see Galen 1944, 124–125). For a reconstruction of the argument, see Kupreeva (2022).

[47] Nasser, Tibi, and Savage-Smith 2009, 8; Stigler 1974.

[48] Boyle did not write to discourage others from making or trusting experiments. On the contrary, the essay offers a number of suggestions for dealing with these contingencies.

had to deal with the variability of plants and dissected bodies, and physicians were faced with variations in their patients' constitutions.

To deal with these many circumstances and contingencies, Boyle recommended that the experimenter "try those Experiments very carefully, and more than once, upon which you mean to build considerable Superstructures either theoretical or practical, and to think it unsafe to rely too much upon single Experiments" (Boyle 1669, 106). A cautious experimenter who performed experimental trials repeatedly had good reason to be confident about their outcomes. Boyle considered repetitions of trials as one of the main precautions in all experimental inquiry, not just in medicine and pharmacology.[49]

This is not the place to examine the history of control strategies in detail, but a few points are worth highlighting. First, the way in which such strategies are implemented and realized may change as the interpretation of control targets changes. Consider the problem of human bias. Experimenters play a double role as subjects and objects of control. As designers of experiments, it is their task to identify possible threats to the validity of experimental results and to make sure they do not affect experimental outcomes. They observe, they record, they check, they select and assign, they randomize, and so forth. Yet experimenters, as human actors doing all these things, may themselves introduce impediments to the experiments. They may be prejudiced or expect certain outcomes, have limited perceptual abilities and attention spans, or may lack the manual skills to carry out a trial. The interpretation of "human bias," its mechanisms and manifestations and of how human observers may interact with experimental processes has changed dramatically over time, and thus also the measures that have been recommended to address it.

Francis Bacon conceptualized human biases as "idols of the mind," as different kinds of illusions that "block men's minds" as he put it in the *Novum Organum* (Bacon 2000, 40). The idols include what we would today describe as limitations of the senses, preoccupations and prejudices, misleading language, and speculative theories. In Boyle's reflections on unsuccessful experiments, he pointed out that fancy, imagination, and prejudice (idols of the cave, in Bacon's typology) may lead to wrong conclusions from experiments. He thus appealed to the experimenters to keep their imaginings in check, as did many other experimenters in the seventeenth and eighteenth centuries. Nineteenth-century researchers, by contrast, often embraced automated recording devices in the hope of obtaining "objective" outcome registrations (Daston and Galison 2007).

[49] In the early eighteenth century, Jakob Bernoulli provided a formal justification for the Law of Large Numbers, according to which events of a certain kind display regularities when there are enough of these events. For the eighteenth- and early-nineteenth-century fate of Bernoulli's theorem, see Hacking (1990, 101–104).

Narratives of the evolution of such strategies could emphasize long-term continuities or situational differences. Boyle's call for self-restraint is a far cry from the automation of observation or from the considerations that lead today's biomedical researchers to design double-blind trials or make random group assignments. But the underlying concern about human experimenters unwittingly distorting empirical evidence is perennial.

Second, canonical experimental approaches – the double-blind RCT, the agricultural trial, placebo studies – are composites of control strategies. Consider, for instance, a double-blind RCT: It involves repetitions (that is, trials on multiple subjects to offset variations among group members), comparisons to establish effects of treatments (whereby members are randomly assigned and only one group receives treatment), and fixing known confounders (blinding the experimenter to prevent selection effects and blinding the subjects to preclude expectations about treatment effects). Agricultural field trials also embody several control strategies; they incorporate repetitions and randomizations as well as direct manipulations of settings. The design of agricultural field trials to test, say, new fertilizers, takes care of multiple contingent, potentially confounding variables, such as incident sunlight, wind exposure, local soil variation, surface irregularities, and so on. Experimenters accomplish this by setting up plots haphazardly around the testing institution which receive fertilizer (or the new fertilizer), and in between there are plots that receive no fertilizer (or the old fertilizer). While each plot has a specific composition of factors, on average, those plots receiving treatments are deemed alike, as are those plots not receiving treatment (or receiving the old treatment) (see Cook and Campbell 1979, 5).

Third, the concrete implementation of control strategies depends heavily on available technologies or technological possibilities. Moreover, like experiments, instruments also play a double role as tools for achieving control over an experimental situation and as potential source of confounders. As tools for achieving control, they are material realizations of what experimenters recognize as conditions and confounders in their experiments. They constrain, record, and measure variables. At the same time, instruments are potential sources of artifacts or systematic distortions of experimental outcomes and thus control targets.

As in the case of human bias, both the understanding and the treatment of instrument-induced distortions have developed substantially, but not always linearly, over time. For instance, microscopes have been in use since the early modern period. Early microscopists were aware of the relation between illumination and image quality and recommended certain precautions such as avoiding direct sunlight as a light source. Theories of optical aberrations in the microscope were developed only during the eighteenth and nineteenth centuries, and even when theoretical interpretations of the instruments were available, they did not directly translate into improved optical properties. Various practical measures, such as the use of test objects, were devised to control the instrument's performance, but they have drawbacks as well.[50]

Fourth, the implementation of control strategies and their perceived effectiveness heavily depends on changing understandings of targets of intervention and control targets. The problem of variation within and across organisms and organic materials has been a constant and particularly challenging management problem in the life sciences. Over the centuries, different kinds of solutions have been developed as the understanding of the source of biological variation changed and as new technologies became available to address it.

Early on, variation reduction was achieved by experimenting on animals or humans deemed sufficiently alike. This practice is evident in James Lind's famous investigations of treatments for scurvy, which he described in his 1753 treatise. Lind made his experiments on twelve sailors suffering from scurvy. The control task, as Lind saw it, was threefold: Similar patients had to be selected, they had to receive differential treatment, and the comparison had to take place against a stable background. Lind accomplished this by selecting patients whose "cases were as similar as I could have them" – which meant, for him, that they had similar symptoms. Limited by the situation on the trip, he had only a small sample of patients to consider. But he did what he could to counter variation across patients and compared them in pairs. Each pair was given the same specific treatment – sea water, lemon, vitriol, and so on – to see which of these treatments was the most effective cure for the disease.[51]

Lind's choices tell us what factors he thought would constitute potential confounders in his experiment – the severity of the symptoms, the environment, the food, and possibly some variable characteristics of the individuals. He designed his experiment such that these factors were held stable across the comparisons as much as possible. His subjects were all in the same environment, they "lay together in one place, being a proper apartment for the sick in the fore-hold," and all ate the same food, "water-gruel sweetened with sugar in the morning; fresh mutton-broth often times for dinner; at other times light puddings, boiled biscuit with sugar, &c. and for supper, barley and raisins, rice and currants, sago and wine, or the like" (Lind 1753, 149).

[50] See Schickore 2009. Aberrations in telescopes posed similar problems. A very expensive confounder is the aberration in the primary mirror of the Hubble space telescope that initially affected the clarity of the telescope's images as it was sent to the sky (DeVorkin and Smith 2011). It took several years of engineering work to fix it.

[51] In the popular literature, Lind's experiment has been hailed as the first controlled clinical trial (e.g. Bartholomew 2002, Bhatt 2010). But as we have seen, Lind simply used a long-standing control strategy.

Spontaneous generation researchers gradually narrowed the scope of their experiments and conclusions to specific – and thus presumably more homogenous – kinds of biotic materials. Twentieth-century life scientists have addressed the problem of variation reduction through working with a few model organisms[52] as well as by producing like organisms through selective breeding and genetic manipulation.

For mid-nineteenth-century physiologist Claude Bernard, even two very similar organisms might not be similar enough for valid comparisons when "delicate and fugitive qualities" are investigated. For Bernard, making comparisons on one and the same animal was an even better way than comparing two similar targets. In situations where delicate qualities were investigated, "we must make our comparison on the same animal, whether the nature of the experiment permit experimenting on him repeatedly at different times, or whether we have to act at one and the same time on similar parts of the same specimen" (Bernard 1957, 128–129). Bernard took this route in his stimulation experiments on frog nerves and muscles. He made the experiment on a pair of legs from one frog, comparing the response of the stimulated leg to the other, which he left untouched. In turn, today's biologists warn that such practice could be problematic because the treatment may spill over and affect the "untreated" part. For instance, if one brain hemisphere is infused with a growth factor and the other side serves as a control, the assumption is that the growth factor does not diffuse to the opposite hemisphere. But if there is no way to check if this assumption holds, using different animals for the experiments is preferable (Lazic, Clarke-Williams, and Munafò 2018).

Finally, the concern raised by these neurobiologists showcases not only the dependence of control task solutions on theoretical understanding and technology but also that, as time passes, seemingly convincing solutions to control problems may be cast into doubt. The neurobiologists point out that the effects of control practices are simply not well enough understood to be considered reliable.

In other contexts, researchers have also raised fundamental concerns about the effectiveness of control strategies. In view of the emphasis Lorraine Daston and Peter Galison have placed on the significance of "mechanical objectivity" for scientific practice, it is worth noting that researchers today express worries about "automation bias," the overreliance on automated recordings for instance in clinical and forensic contexts (Goddard, Roudsari, and Wyatt 2012).

[52] The crucial role of model organisms for the modern life sciences, the details of their production, and the communities that have formed around them have been well studied (see, e.g., Rader 2004, Ankeny and Leonelli 2020).

Control practices may even be detrimental if they "over-control" the experiment so much that the results no longer apply to natural environments or organisms. Reliance on standardized "factory mice" in biomedical research may limit what one can learn about diseases like Parkinson's or stroke (Engber 2013). Using pristine and standardized plastic pellets in studies of environmental hazards by microplastics instead of aged, irregularly shaped plastic bits impedes studies of the environmental impact of these materials (Kühn et al. 2018, Rozman and Kalčíková 2022). In public health research, control typically needs to be balanced with other demands on research design. Researchers must overcome barriers for recruitment, attrition, or sample size, which may necessitate lowering the bar for subject selection to gather any valuable information at all (Crosby et al. 2010).

6 Making Controlled Experiments

6.1 Confounder Repertoires

The most fundamental control problem is the management of background factors in the less-than-ideal situations that experimenters confront in actual scientific inquiry. But how does one establish what things need to be controlled in a given situation?

According to William Wimsatt, nothing general or abstract can be said about designing experimental controls; "there are no universal control setups. What one must control is a function of what relationships one is studying" (Wimsatt 2007, 84). In other words, it is the experimenters' task to determine what control targets they need to worry about in their specific research contexts. Experimenters (or their successors, or we analysts of science) figure out in retrospect whether there were control targets that were not appropriately handled.

In many cases, however, researchers can rely on a stock of control targets deemed relevant for their research area. Evolutionary epistemologist and social scientist Donald Campbell and psychologist Julian Stanley put together a list of factors that they considered most important for educational studies. If not controlled, these factors threaten the validity of experimental studies in educational research (Campbell and Stanley 1966, 5–6, see also Campbell 1957). The experimental designs they described acknowledge experimenters' lack of complete control over the experimental setting and environment.[53] Some items on their list apply to virtually all comparative trials involving groups of human subjects,

[53] They turn against an ideal according to which "an experimenter having complete mastery can schedule treatments and measurements for optimal statistical efficiency, with complexity of design emerging only from that goal of efficiency" (Campbell and Stanley 1966). They associate this ideal with R. A. Fisher's work.

such as selection bias in group assignments or the differential loss of group members through attrition. Others are more specific to social research, such as "history," that is, the influence on the subjects of current events between an initial and a later measurement, or "maturation," that is, the physiological changes of the subjects due to the passing of time between the first and later trials (growing older, growing tired, and so on).[54] The factor "history," for instance, can be addressed by running sessions with experimental and control groups simultaneously, as members of both groups would be equally affected by current events – although, as Campbell and Stanley noted, one would have to employ different experimenters, and "experimenter differences can become a form of intrasession history confounded with *X* [the treatment]" (Campbell and Stanley 1966, 14). Actual study designs involve tradeoffs among various control practices.

Campbell and Stanley considered field-specific control targets. Philosopher of neuroscience Jaqueline Sullivan has proposed a more project-centered approach. She has plausibly argued that research projects within a certain field – operant conditioning in rodents, in her case – typically come with repertoires of potential confounders, or "confounds," as she calls them. These confounder repertoires comprise all the things that must be controlled in that project.[55] To build such repertoires and determine what needs to be controlled in an experimental project, scientists can and do rely on "fundamental and routine parts of the research landscape and culture" (Sullivan 2022, 3).[56]

Project-specific repertoires of confounders include a diverse set of issues deemed relevant for the study, some more common, others specific to a particular experimental setup. In research on operant conditioning, the repertoire includes distracting sounds, lack of motivation on the part of the rat, investigator bias, investigator–animal interaction, and so on. The corresponding control tasks are similarly diverse, comprising soundproofing the testing chamber, using a food-restrictive diet to ensure motivation in reward-based learning,

[54] This factor is also relevant for biomedical research, where some animals, fruit flies for instance, age significantly during the experiment.

[55] The term "confounder repertoire" resonates with Deborah Mayo's "error repertoire," although an error repertoire is more general in scope than a confounder repertoire. An error repertoire is a trans-contextual catalog of canonical errors, relevant to virtually all research. It includes common types of experimental mistakes, such as mistaking artifacts for real effects, mistakes about causal factors, or mistakes about the value of a parameter (Mayo 1996, 17–18). In the context of experimental control, the notion of confounder is preferable to the notion of error because the presence of confounders does not necessarily lead to erroneous results. Confounders may confuse, and no result can be obtained.

[56] I noted in the introduction that numerous manuals for laboratory research are commercially available. It would be very interesting to examine whether these manuals are routinely used and, if so, whether they indeed facilitate solving control problems in laboratory practice.

and computerized automatization to eliminate experimenter errors and biases (Sullivan 2022, 5).

Some of the control targets in Sullivan's example are canonical. They are part of the broader research culture of, say, neurobiology or developmental psychology (or even biology or psychology). Others are specific to the research task at hand. Using a food-restrictive diet to ensure motivation is not exclusive to the touchscreen experiments, not even to neuroscience. It is common in reward-based learning experiments with animals. The placement of the food dispenser relative to the touchscreen, by contrast, is specific to the touchscreen study Sullivan analyzes. The placement is crucial for determining what exactly the rodents are learning in the experiment (Sullivan 2022, 5). Control problems within such a study include many default issues that experimenters expect to come up in neurobiological experimentation as well as certain default ways to address them. What one must control is thus not entirely a function of the relationship one is studying but also informed by discipline-specific, and sometimes long-standing routines.

Of course, whether one can consider control targets or confounders as project-specific, field-specific, or general crucially depends on the level of resolution at which one describes those projects. Consider again spontaneous generation research. It is a fundamental and routine part of spontaneous generation research to exclude contaminating biotic materials from experimental settings. Building well-sealed flasks and developing procedures to purify or sterilize (as it came to be called) the fluid in them are fundamental and routine parts of virtually all spontaneous generation experiments. Emphasizing the long-term perspective, one could say, for instance, that Tyndall was, as everyone else, concerned with shielding his samples from contaminations. But it is equally plausible to say that Tyndall was addressing quite specific control problems due to the nature of the contaminants with which he was dealing. Those endospores that puzzled Tyndall required specific management because of their heat-resistance, and this was one of the distinctive features of his research.

The epistemologically relevant point is that in fields with established experimental traditions, experimenters routinely ascertain what it is that needs to be controlled in concrete experiments. But these routines do not fully and conclusively determine the confounder repertoire for a project even in established fields. After all, in rodent operant conditioning research, it has taken many years of work by several research groups to develop and tweak the tools and detectors and to optimize the control of the experiment, and it is conceivable that they could have found a different way of accomplishing this. And in situations when researchers venture out into completely new fields of experimentation, when very little is known about the phenomena of interest, it is indeed plausible to say that objects of study and control targets emerge together as the experimenters develop the project. Experimenters seeking to build confounder repertoires for their experiments may not even know where to begin their search.[57]

6.2 The Making of Controlled Experiments

Throughout this Element, I have emphasized that dealing with control targets is both a conceptual and a technical-practical task. On a conceptual level, investigators identify and distinguish various background factors that are possibly relevant in bringing about, modifying, or preventing an effect. On the practical level, technical solutions must be found to address control issues. This can be a complicated, time-consuming process.

Past researchers often shared details of their efforts to work through control problems. In today's published experimental reports, there is typically little textual evidence of these endeavors. In the case of operant conditioning research, the activities involved in working through control problems are rendered visible because an analyst (Sullivan) has been a participant observer in the neurobiological laboratory.

Building suitable project-specific confounder repertoires and developing the technologies to harness control targets can take a long time. Claude Bernard made this point in his discussion of comparative trials (which, as we have seen, require harnessing background factors). He characterized comparative experimentation as a *process* of exploration and pursuit. The experimenter who examines an object or phenomenon "proceeds by differentiation, that is to say, he separates each of these bodies, one by one in succession, and sees by the difference what part of the total phenomenon belongs to each of them" (Bernard 1957, 127). In building a confounder repertoire, experimenters first examine as systematically as possible what factors contribute what to a phenomenon of interest. Only when this is accomplished can one establish whether an assumption about the relation between a phenomenon of interest and its putative cause is indeed correct.

Bernard took the occasion to argue that comparative experimentation in physiology is less rigorous than in physics because an investigator's ability to proceed "by differentiation" in the manner described is more limited. Physiological phenomena, Bernard noted, "are so complex that we could never experiment at all rigorously on living animals if we necessarily had to

[57] In a recent publication (Schickore 2019), I used the terms "diagnostic" and "determinative probing" to distinguish between the two tasks of building a confounder repertoire and of controlling for these confounders in a given experimental situation. I now think that the labels I chose are a little confusing. The distinction itself, however, is important, as this and the next section show.

define all the other changes we might cause in the organism on which we were operating" (Bernard 1957, 127–128). Instead, biomedical experimenters resort to what we would today call "sham operations," a process that Bernard described as "adding to a similar organism, used for comparison, all our experimental changes save one, the very one which we intend to disengage" (Bernard 1957, 128). He introduced such sham operations as a means to avoid confusion between the effects of lesions caused by an operative procedure and the section or ablation of an organ whose role the experimenter wishes to study.

Solutions to control problems depend and rely on technological possibilities. In the case of rodent research, some technical problems – how to separate the cognitive stimulus from the food reward, for example – were easy to address by tweaking the setup of the touch-screen experiments. In other cases, the solution may not be so straightforward. The history of the spontaneous generation debates shows that even if all investigators agree what the background factors are that need to be controlled, the technical problems that need to be solved do not have obvious solutions.

Finding solutions to control problems requires theoretical assumptions, as spontaneous generation research amply illustrates. Similarly, the neurobiologists who are concerned about spillover effects from treated to untreated parts of the brain (Section 5) base their concerns on assumptions about brain functions, and on this basis, they judge comparative trials on one and the same organism as insufficiently controlled.

Technical solutions to control problems also involve some theoretical understanding – at times substantial theoretical understanding – of how putative confounders interact with the setting.[58] The elaborate devices that Pasteur, Schulze, and Tyndall developed and built to purify the air before it reaches an infusion were technological feats, but they also relied on theoretical assumptions about what kinds of biotic materials might contaminate their samples and how to manipulate these invisible things.

In addition, finding solutions to control problems can be tricky because certain phenomena are not easily tractable. Markus Eronen has discussed the difficulties that psychological researchers face as they seek to control their experiments. He has demonstrated in detail that in psychological experimentation, there is "no straightforward way of manipulating or changing the values of psychological variables (as in, for example, electrical circuits or drug trials). Interventions in psychology have to be done, for example, through verbal

[58] Boring called attention to the point that controls require hypotheses: "When there is no acceptable hypothesis as to the independent variable in an experiment, it may be impossible to have a control, which may become available only when a good hypothesis comes along" (Boring 1954, 582).

information . . . or through visual/auditory stimuli, and such manipulations are not precise enough to manipulate just one psychological variable" (Eronen 2020). Measurements of these variables are typically based on self-reports, so there is uncertainty about what exactly the dependent variable is. For similar reasons, it is hard to see how the experimenter or the experimental subject can hold fixed psychological factors such as mental states, emotions, or thoughts.

Consider the research on the Mozart effect, the hypothesized causal influence that listening to Mozart has on children's IQ (Feest 2019). What is the target system in this case, and what are the factors that should be controlled in an experiment examining the Mozart effect? Does it matter whether the piece is played slow or fast, whether it is a symphony, an opera, or a piano sonata, whether it is long or short, how often the child is exposed to it, whether the child has musical training (and if the latter, would the measured effect be due to the training or the listening)? Or can all these features be safely ignored? Uljana Feest has called these kinds of determinations "individuation judgments." They determine what target system is, what background is, and what extraneous is to the study. As noted in Section 3, these determinations are relational. The point is that there are no definitively correct individuation judgments to make. But once these judgments are made, they shape the knowledge that is gained in this experiment. In this case, what is controlled is indeed mostly a function of what one is studying.

Making individuation judgments is importantly a collective endeavor. In the case of the Mozart effect, several different experimenters argued about the appropriateness of judgments and decisions in light of accepted disciplinary knowledge. The collective negotiation of control tasks can be productive in that it can lead not only to solutions of control problems but also to the emergence of new control tasks. When various groups in the community start using a new apparatus, it frequently happens that new control problems become apparent and necessitate changes of the setting to address or eliminate them. In the operant conditioning experiments, for instance, systematic confounders came into view only at a later stage in the project, notably the problem of potential visual stimulus bias. Initially, the reward was delivered in food cups below the touchscreen. In this arrangement, it was not clear to which stimulus the rats responded. Separating the touchscreen and the dispenser was deemed crucial for determining what exactly the rodents were learning in the experiment (Sullivan 2022, 5). This change, as well as various other modifications of the apparatus to refine the stimuli and direct the rats' behavior, made it possible to determine what exactly the rodents were learning in the experiment. Over time, the apparatus and procedures were stabilized. The setup became a well-ordered tool to investigate the links between neural activity and behavior in rodents.

Feest's discussion of the Mozart effect illustrates both how flexible and how consequential decisions about control tasks can be in psychological experimentation. The selection of what is being manipulated and measured, the judgments about what the relevant features of these factors are, and the complement, what the confounding factors are, have what Feest calls "a high degree of epistemic uncertainty" (Feest 2019, 897).[59] At the same time, these decisions are crucial and in fact constitutive of the knowledge that can be gained in the experiment.

This process of establishing control tasks is not always linear such that, as research progresses, experimenters gradually pinpoint a target system while figuring out more things to control. Sometimes the designations of putative confounders and target systems change drastically. The history of spontaneous generation research illustrates this more general point. Projects shifted and transformed as the understanding of life and living matter evolved and as potential control targets were explored experimentally. Each researcher in the spontaneous generation debates had to deal with the stabilization of background factors. But what these conditions were thought to be, how they were understood to impact the experiment, and thus how they could be managed, changed dramatically. The researchers went from excluding flies to excluding dust; from killing by boiling to killing by fractional boiling; from visible to instrumentally detectable to conjectural entities that need to be handled.

On shorter timescales, control targets can change significantly; and previously unconceived factors become incorporated in the causal nexus under study. In Section 4.2, I showed how parts of the equipment in the most recent spontaneous generation experiments – the borosilicate in the Teflon flasks – became part of the target system. Consider also a recent example from photosynthesis research (Stasinopoulos and Hangarter 1990, Hangarter and Stasinopoulos 1991). Plant tissues and cells are usually grown on defined media in which the chemical nature and the quantities of all components are known when the media are first prepared. The growth of cultured plant tissues is determined by the initial levels of growth substances and nutrients in the culture medium as well as by the relative rates of their disappearance as the plant grows. For a long time, it was assumed that blue and near-UV light, well-known inhibitors of elongation growth in seedlings, would act on light-sensitive systems in the plant tissues. However, experimental study on the model organism Arabidopsis revealed that the growth inhibition was primarily due to photochemical alterations of the culture medium rather than to photosensory functions of the plant tissue itself. When culture media are exposed to plant material, the medium composition

[59] The article discusses replication rather than control, but as successful replication presupposes successful control, Feest's examples lend itself to my purposes.

changes as cells metabolize components. Moreover, abiotic factors such as light and heat can change the chemical composition of culture media as well. In studies of plant metabolism, both of these factors affect plant growth and must be appropriately monitored, as it turned out.

A most dramatic development that demonstrates both the constitutive role and the revisability of experimental control tasks is the investigation of bisphenol-A exposure in mice (Landecker 2013). The initial experiments were on the biology of infertility. In these experiments, mouse strains were used that had unusually high numbers of chromosomal abnormalities resulting from aberrant meiosis. These were compared with control mice not carrying the mutant genotype. However, as the experiments went on, 40 percent of the control mice showed failures of chromosomal alignment during meiosis. The researchers determined that the features of the setting were in fact influencing the experimental process: The plastic cages and plastic water bottles used in the experiment had been washed with detergent and sterilized at high heat, which led to bisphenol-A leakage from the plastic. The mice would ingest the chemical and absorb it through their skin. In subsequent experiments, the impact on the reproductive process of bisphenol-A became the focus of the study, and the erstwhile "control mouse" became the experimental animal. This is more than just a reversal of experimental and control case. The entire research project shifted, and researchers eventually conducted their studies on animals *within* an environment.[60]

Over time, the understanding of what factors should be kept fixed or monitored in experimental practice may change fundamentally even within one and the same research field. The relation between target system and background factors may be recast, and factors previously considered extraneous to the experiment may become recognized as relevant background.

All these issues – that potentially confounding factors must be identified, that this process is partly shaped by routines, that these choices have a degree of epistemic uncertainty, that the identification likely depends on both theoretical assumptions and technical possibilities, and that the choices are made over time and are reversible – also apply to the design of controls in a comparative experiment.

A control is typically not an organism in its natural state or "nature taking its course." Rather, it is a designed thing or process, made to resemble the experimental case as closely as possible in respects deemed relevant in the particular research context. A "wild type" used for comparison in genetic research is not an organism found in the wild but a laboratory animal selectively inbred and isolated from wild populations (Holmes 2017). A "control mouse" used in the

[60] See also Landecker (2016) for a similar episode.

investigation of autoimmune diseases is not a common domestic or field mouse but a laboratory mouse specifically designed for the purpose of studying autoimmune responses.

There are various different ways to design the control mice even within that particular context of autoimmune response research, either by inbreeding or by engineering the genome. In genetic engineering, a specific gene can be over-expressed or eliminated. The design of the appropriate control mouse not only depends on which of these engineering approaches is used but also on a thorough understanding of the effects of the genetic manipulation in the organism that is studied. Notably, if a gene of interest is injected into a fertilized egg, it may modify the expression of the gene into which it integrates, potentially modifying one of the genes that are involved in auto-immune disease susceptibility. Since the injected gene is assumed to integrate randomly, uncertainty ensues in the construction of the control case (Morel 2004, e424).[61]

Finally, figuring out the relevant background factors for an experiment and the possible sources of variation in target systems itself involves experimentation – second-order experiments, experiments on experiments – whereby experimenters explore what the factors are that make a difference to the experimental outcomes and what difference they make. Inspired by Feest, we could characterize these second-order experiments as "individuation experiments." As we saw in Section 4, several spontaneous generation researchers engaged in extensive projects of this sort. As noted, this kind of second-order experimentation is a key component of designing controlled experiments. What I have said about controlled experimentation also applies to second-order experimentation.

Identifying and specifying control targets experimentally often involves complicated instruments as well as theoretical arguments by which the success or failure of the second-order experiment can be demonstrated. In the case of spontaneous generation research, experimenters probed background factors extensively with second-order experiments using inventions such as high-power blowpipes or windowed dust-free boxed. Good experimental methods including controls are required for these second-order experiments as well. Each potentially relevant causal factor should be investigated and compared with a control case to establish whether it might influence the experimental process. And as in first-order experimentation, the second-order experiments are not perfectly controlled experiments and may not be decisive.

[61] Morel notes that this confounding factor is usually addressed by producing and comparing several transgenic lines (Morel 2004, e424).

As we have seen throughout this Element, the determination of the content of a confounder repertoire is both technical-practical and conceptual and importantly an experimental and social process. It requires alignment of theoretical ideas and arguments, techniques, equipment, and skills. Moreover, even if everyone agrees about what needs to be controlled in a concrete research context, the technical problems arising do not have obvious solutions. Confounder repertoires take shape over time, as the experimenters conduct their research. They are also revisable; a repertoire can change significantly as the project develops. Science's past is full of examples that can be explored further to illustrate these points.[62]

I titled this section "Making Controlled Experiments." The title exploits the double meaning of the term "making": making in the sense of carrying out a task or doing something and making in the sense of manufacturing a product. Both meanings are relevant for understanding the role and function of control in experimentation. There are both conceptual and technical tasks involved in the process, and it has an experimental component. There is a degree of freedom in this process, and at the same time, its results are crucial for experimental learning. Not every choice concerning confounder repertoires is a plausible choice, but nevertheless, there may be reasonable disagreement about the composition and comprehensiveness of these repertoires for particular experiments.

In sum, what must be controlled, and how, is partly, but not wholly, a function of what one is studying. Experimental control is at the same time constitutive of the knowledge that can be gained in an experiment and a function of tradition, of situated decisions, of available background knowledge and technical possibilities, of second-order experimentation, and subject of interactions between research group members and between research groups.

7 Understanding Experimental Control Epistemologically, Pragmatically, and Historically

Control is commonly associated with stability and order. Both in the context of experimentation and beyond, controlling a thing or process means reigning it in, keeping it in check. It also means checking and verifying, making sure *that* order and stability have been achieved and are maintained. Experimental control understood as check and verification happens after an experiment is designed and potential confounding factors have been identified. With adequate

[62] See the contributions to Schickore and Newman (2024) for several accounts exemplifying transformations of control problems, including in eighteenth-century plant physiology (Schürch 2024); nineteenth-century psychic research (Cristalli 2024); and twentieth-century studies of animal behavior (Arnet 2024).

controls in place, the experimental outcomes license the causal claims under investigation.

This Element has examined what is involved in achieving and maintaining order and what obstacles and limitations arise. It has focused on the historical and technical-practical dimensions of experimental control and has argued that only if we examine how experimental control comes into being can we fully understand its role in experimental inquiry. Most importantly, my account has shifted the attention from control experiments, comparative trials, to the broader issue of the management of background factors. Control experiments are what first come to mind when we think about control in experimental practice. But controlling for background factors is the epistemologically fundamental issue in controlled experimentation. Therefore, I have given the issue of "controlling for" background factors more room than the discussion of "control experiment" – the comparison with a control case.

Historically informed philosophical analysis of scientific practice can be done in different ways, at different levels of scale – up close, in depth, and in short durée; from a bird's-eye view and in long durée; and from a middle ground and with an eye to medium-term duration. With regard to controlled experimentation, the analysis may emphasize the continuities, the perennial control strategies, or the specificities of the tasks scientists need to address in specific situations. The need to control for human bias is enduring and recurrent, but there is room for different implementations and realizations. Implementing and realizing is a collective, extended process of pursuit. It often involves second-order experiments on the tools and the environment in which the experiment is happening.

In experimental control, the technical and the conceptual are intertwined. The technical problems arising from the desire to control do not have straightforward, obvious solutions. How they are solved is contingent on available knowledge, skills, and materials. At the same time, the solutions are constitutive for the knowledge that can be gained in the experiment.

Intuitively, we might be inclined to say that modern science is far better controlled than past science. Technical improvements – increase in speed, practicality, or precision – occur frequently in the history of science. Scientists today have labs, standardized materials, and sophisticated instruments to investigate the inner workings of organisms, even techniques to engineer their experimental targets. We have genetic scissors such as CRISPR-cas9, which are precise tools for making targeted interventions on an organism's DNA. Precision instruments, elaborate recording devices, and other technologies that became available in the last century or two can assist with control tasks and, one may assume, make it easier to keep an experimental situation stable and to track changes of interest.

If we consider how the tools and techniques for control come into being, however, it appears that modern experiments are often harder to control precisely because scientific instrumentation has advanced so vastly. Identifying what to control involves decisions under uncertainty, which, once the decisions are made, are constitutive of the knowledge gained in the project. This explains why scientists refer to experimental controls both as extremely important parts of their experiments and as extremely difficult to figure out. The quote with which this Element started highlights the openness of the control process. There is no universal stock of experimental controls, ready to use in every experiment. Just as there is no recipe for generating new scientific ideas, there is no recipe for arriving at ideas about what to control in an experiment. Still, in hindsight, it is possible to see that the articulation of experimental controls, like experimentation itself, does not happen in a vacuum. Scientists rely on their previous knowledge, experience, and technology to identify relevant background factors and ways to deal with them.

Consider once more the spontaneous generation experiments. Arguably, for Redi's specific purposes, the control he had achieved over his jars, pieces of meat, and flies was sufficient to warrant the causal conclusions he wanted to draw. Compared to Redi (and Needham and Spallanzani), the nineteenth-century investigators used much more sophisticated instruments, sometimes exploiting up-to-date technologies from other scientific fields. But more advanced instrumentation does not necessarily equal more control. In Redi's experiments, the success of the screening process could be checked by observation. Unlike Redi's flies, the potential contaminants that later researchers suspected might be present in infusions or in the air cannot be directly manipulated. Nineteenth-century experimenters built ingenious apparatuses they deemed suitable for cleansing air from invisible matter whose existence and qualities they could only assume. At the same time, keeping all potentially relevant factors "under control" became more difficult, and tradeoffs were often necessary.

Schulze's repurposed *Kaliapparat*, Tyndall's dust chamber, and Pasteur's iconic flasks help manipulate invisible things. These contraptions are the material realizations of what the experimenters recognized as the relevant confounders for their experiments, and they keep those confounders in check. But such devices need to be controlled themselves. The technologies to screen off contaminants get increasingly complicated, to a point where the proper functioning of the apparatus itself becomes a problem to be addressed. Instrumentation might even introduce additional factors that require tracking or might impede the process of experimentation.

In biomedical experimentation, complex and variable living things pose extra challenges to the experimenter. Notably, as we saw in Section 5, adequately controlling an experiment in biomedical research may also mean forestalling too much organization and management. The background is as difficult to treat as the target system, both conceptually and in actual experimental practice. At the same time, it is urgent to get it right, as the lives and well-being of humans and animals (and the reputation of the researchers) depend on the results. The question of whether the instruments do what we think, or hope, they do is in part a theoretical question, at least until the instrument becomes established as a routine tool. As background factors and targets of intervention become increasingly remote from everyday experience, the checks the experimenters apply become less immediate and more dependent on various, potentially faulty assumptions about the functioning of their instruments and techniques. The fervent debates between Needham and Spallanzani and between Bastian and Tyndall illustrate that it is by no means easy to decide whether a technical solution to a practical problem – boiling an infusion, for instance – works reliably enough to be considered satisfying. For more complex instruments, the question of whether control succeeds is both a practical and a theoretical one. Experimental control involves aligning knowledge and arguments, techniques, equipment, and skills.

Experimental control is at the same time informed by history and contingent on a concrete research situation. There are no universal control procedures and no recipes for designing project-specific confounder repertoires, but there are traditions of dealing with control issues. The fundamental strategies are perennial; the more specific control practices develop and change, they are handed down, improved, revised, and sometimes replaced by new ones. What must be controlled, and how, is worked out anew for every project, often collectively but not from scratch – it is done partly by mobilizing long-standing methodological ideas and available technologies, partly by making contingent decisions, partly by second-order experimentation. The stability thus achieved is temporary and revisable, but also historically shaped. For this reason, historical reflection is a crucial element of analyzing controlled experimentation.

References

Allchin, Douglas. 2020. "The Counter-Roll in Science." *The American Biology Teacher* 82: 188–191.

Ankeny, Rachel A., and Sabina Leonelli. 2020. *Model Organisms*. Cambridge Elements. Cambridge: Cambridge University Press.

Arnet, Evan. 2024. "Controlling away the Phenomenon: Maze Research and the Nature of Learning." In *Elusive Phenomena, Unwieldy Things: Historical Perspectives on Experimental Control*, edited by Jutta Schickore and William R. Newman. Cham: Springer.

Bacon, Francis. 2000. *The New Organon*. Cambridge: Cambridge University Press.

Bartholomew, M. 2002. "James Lind's Treatise of the Scurvy (1753)." *Postgraduate Medical Journal* 78: 695–696.

Beebee, Helen, Christopher Hitchcock, and Peter Menzies, eds. 2009. *The Oxford Handbook of Causation*. Oxford: Oxford University Press.

Bernard, Claude. 1957. *An Introduction to the Study of Experimental Medicine*. New York: Dover. 1865.

Bertoloni Meli, Domenico. 2009. "A Lofty Mountain, Putrefying Flesh, Styptic Water, and Germinating Seeds." In *The Accademia del Cimento and Its European Context*, edited by Marco Beretta, Antonio Clericuzio, and Larry Principe, 121–134. Sagamore Beach: Science History.

Bhatt, Arun. 2010. "Evolution of Clinical Research: A History before and beyond James Lind." *Perspectives in Clinical Research* 1: 6–10.

Boring, Edwin Garrigues. 1954. "The Nature and History of Experimental Control." *American Journal of Psychology* 67: 573–589.

Boyle, Robert. 1669. *Certain Physiological Essays and Other Tracts: Written at distant Times, and on Several Occasions*. 2nd ed. London: Printed for Henry Herringman at the Blew Anchor.

Campbell, Donald T. 1957. "Factors Relevant to the Validity of Experiments in Social Settings." *Psychological Bulletin* 54 (4): 297–312. https://doi.org/10.1037/h0040950.

Campbell, Donald T., and Julian C. Stanley. 1966. *Experimental and Quasi-Experimental Designs for Research*. Chicago: Rand McNally.

Cartwright, Nancy. 2007. "Are RCTs the Gold Standard?" *Bio Societies* 2: 11–20.

2010. "What Are Randomised Controlled Trials Good for?" *Philosophical Studies* 147 (1): 59–70. https://doi.org/10.1007/s11098-009-9450-2.

2011. "The Art of Medicine: A Philosopher's View of the Long Road from RCTs to Effectiveness." *Lancet* 377: 1400–1401.

Chang, Hasok. 2022. *Realism for Realistic People: A New Pragmatist Philosophy of Science*. Cambridge: Cambridge University Press.

Cinelli, Carlos, Andrew Forney, and Judea Pearl. 2022. "A Crash Course in Good and Bad Controls." *Sociological Methods & Research*. https://ssrn.com/abstract=3689437.

Cohn, Ferdinand. 1872. "Untersuchungen über Bacterien." *Beiträge zur Biologie der Pflanzen* I (2): 127–244.

Conant, James B. 1961. *Science and Common Sense*. 2nd printing. New Haven: Yale University Press. 1951.

Cook, Thomas D., and Donald T. Campbell. 1979. *Quasi-Experimentation: Design and Analysis Issues for Field Settings*. Boston: Houghton Mifflin Boston.

Criado-Reyes, Joaquín, Bruno M. Bizzarri, Juan Manuel García-Ruiz, et al. 2021. "The Role of Borosilicate Glass in Miller–Urey Experiment." *Scientific Reports* 11, 21009. https://doi.org/10.1038/s41598-021-00235-4.

Cristalli, Claudia. 2024. "A 'Careful Examination of All Kind of Phenomena': Methodology and Psychical Research at the End of the Nineteenth Century." In *Elusive Phenomena, Unwieldy Things: Historical Perspectives on Experimental Control*, edited by Jutta Schickore and William R. Newman. Cham: Springer.

Crosby, Richard, Laura F. Salazar, Ralph DiClemente, and Delia Lang. 2010. "Balancing Rigor against the Inherent Limitations of Investigating Hard-to-Reach Populations." *Health Education Research* 25: 1–5.

Curry, Helen. 2016. *Evolution Made to Order*. Chicago: University of Chicago Press.

Daston, Lorraine, and Peter Galison. 2007. *Objectivity*. Boston: Zone Books.

DeVorkin, David H., and Robert W. Smith. 2011. *Hubble: Imaging Space and Time*. 1st pbk. print. ed. Washington, D.C.: National Geographic.

Eberhardt, Frederick, and Richard Scheines. 2007. "Interventions and Causal Inference." *Philosophy of Science* 74 (5): 981–995. https://doi.org/10.1086/525638.

Engber, Daniel. 2013. "The Mouse Trap: How One Rodent Rules the Lab." *Slate*. www.slate.com/articles/health_and_science/the_mouse_trap/2011/11/the_mouse_trap.html.

Eronen, Markus I. 2020. "Causal Discovery and the Problem of Psychological Interventions." *New Ideas in Psychology* 59: 100785. https://doi.org/10.1016/j.newideapsych.2020.100785.

Farley, John. 1977. *The Spontaneous Generation Controversy from Descartes to Oparin*. Baltimore: Johns Hopkins University Press.

Feest, Uljana. 2019. "Why Replication Is Overrated." *Philosophy of Science* 86: 895–905.

Fenton-Glynn, Luke. 2021. *Causation*. Cambridge: Cambridge University Press

Foucault, Michel. 1975. *The Birth of the Clinic: An Archaeology of Medical Perception*. New York: Vintage Books.

1979. *Discipline and Punish: The Birth of the Prison*. New York: Vintage.

Fuller, J. 2019. "The Confounding Question of Confounding Causes in Randomized Trials." *British Journal for the Philosophy of Science* 70 (3): 901–926. https://doi.org/10.1093/bjps/axx015.

Galen. 1944. *Galen on Medical Experience*. 1st ed. of the Arabic ed. New York [etc.]: Pub. for the trustees of the late Sir Henry Wellcome by the Oxford University Press.

Galison, Peter. 2010. "Secrecy in Three Acts." *Social Research: An International Quarterly* 77: 941–974.

Gallow, J. Dmitri. 2022. "The Metaphysics of Causation." In *The Stanford Encyclopedia of Philosophy*, edited by Edward N. Zalta and Uri Nodelman. https://plato.stanford.edu/archives/fall2022/entries/causation-metaphysics/.

Geison, Gerald. 1995. *The Private Science of Louis Pasteur*. Princeton: Princeton University Press.

Gigerenzer, Gerd, Zeno G. Swijtink, Theodore M. Porter, et al. 1989. *The Empire of Chance: How Probability Changed Science and Everyday Life*. Cambridge: Cambridge University Press.

Goddard, Kate, Abdul Roudsari, and Jeremy C. Wyatt. 2012. "Automation Bias: A Systematic Review of Frequency, Effect Mediators, and Mitigators." *Journal of the American Medical Informatics Association* 19 (1): 121–127. https://doi.org/10.1136/amiajnl-2011-000089.

Grice, Herbert Paul. 1989. *Studies in the Way of Words*. Cambridge: Harvard University Press.

Guala, Francesco. 2005. *The Methodology of Experimental Economics*. Cambridge: Cambridge University Press.

Hacking, Ian. 1988. "Telepathy: Origins of Randomization in Experimental Design" *Isis* 79: 427–451.

1990. *The Taming of Chance*. Cambridge: Cambridge University Press.

Hangarter, Roger P., and Triant C. Stasinopoulos. 1991. "Repression of Plant Tissue Culture Growth by Light Is Caused by Photochemical Change in the Culture Medium." *Plant Science* 79 (2): 253–257. https://doi.org/10.1016/0168-9452(91)90114-N.

Hernán, Miguel A., Sonia Hernández-Díaz, Martha M. Werler, and Allen A. Mitchell. 2002. "Causal Knowledge as a Prerequisite for Confounding Evaluation: An Application to Birth Defects Epidemiology." *American Journal of Epidemiology* 155 (2): 176–84. https://doi.org/10.1093/aje/155.2.176.

Hoffmann, Christoph. 2001. "The Design of Disturbance: Physics Institutes and Physics Research in Germany, 1870–1910." *Perspectives on Science* 9: 173–195.

Holman, Bennett. 2020. "Humbug, the Council of Pharmacy and Chemistry, and the Origin of 'The Blind Test' of Therapeutic Efficacy." In *Uncertainty in Pharmacology: Epistemology, Methods and Decisions*, edited by Barbara Osimani and Adam LaCaze, 397–416. Dordrecht: Springer.

Holmes, Tarquin. 2017. "The Wild Type as Concept and in Experimental Practice: A History of Its Role in Classical Genetics and Evolutionary Theory." *Studies in History and Philosophy of Biological and Biomedical Sciences* 63: 15–27. https://doi.org/10.1016/j.shpsc.2017.03.006.

Hough, L. and A. F. Rogers. 1956. "Synthesis of Amino-Acids from Water, Hydrogen, Methane and Ammonia." *Journal of Physiology* 132 (2): 28–30p.

Illari, Phyllis, and Federica Russo. 2014. *Causality: Philosophical Theory Meets Scientific Practice*. Oxford: Oxford University Press.

Krauss, Alexander. 2021. "Assessing the Overall Validity of Randomised Controlled Trials." *International Studies in the Philosophy of Science* 34 (3): 159–182. https://doi.org/10.1080/02698595.2021.2002676.

Kühn, Susanne, Albert van Oyen, Andy Booth, André Meijboom, and Jan A. van Franeker. 2018. "Marine Microplastic: Preparation of Relevant Test Materials for Laboratory Assessment of Ecosystem Impacts." *Chemosphere* 213: 103–113. https://doi.org/10.1016/j.chemosphere.2018.09.032.

Kupreeva, Inna. 2022. "Galen's Empiricist Background: A Study of the Argument in On Medical Experience." In *Galen's Epistemology: Experience, Reason, and Method in Ancient Medicine*, edited by Matyáš Havrda and Robert J. Hankinson, 32–78. Cambridge: Cambridge University Press.

Landecker, Hannah. 2013. "When the Control Becomes the Experiment." *Limn* 3: 6–8.

2016. "It Is What It Eats: Chemically Defined Media and the History of Surrounds." *Studies in History and Philosophy of Biological and Biomedical Sciences* 57: 148–160.

Lazcano, Antonio, and Jeffrey L. Bada. 2003. "The 1953 Stanley L. Miller Experiment: Fifty Years of Prebiotic Organic Chemistry." *Origins of Life and Evolution of the Biosphere* 33 (3): 235–242. https://doi.org/10.1023/A:1024807125069.

Lazcano, Antonio, and Stanley L. Miller. 1996. "The Origin and Early Evolution of Life: Prebiotic Chemistry, the Pre-RNA World, and Time." *Cell* 85 (6): 793–798. https://doi.org/10.1016/s0092-8674(00)81263-5.

Lazic, Stanley. E., Charlie J. Clarke-Williams, and Marcus R. Munafò. 2018. "What Exactly Is 'N' in Cell Culture and Animal Experiments?" *PLoS Biology* 16 (4): 1–14. e2005282. https://doi.org/10.1371/journal.pbio.2005282.

Lehman, Christine, and Bernadette Bensaude-Vincent. 2007. "Public Demonstrations of Chemistry in Eighteenth Century France." *Science & Education* 16 (6): 573–583. https://doi.org/10.1007/s11191-006-9025-y.

Lehoux, Daryn. 2017. *Creatures Born of Mud and Slime: The Wonder and Complexity of Spontaneous Generation*. Baltimore: Johns Hopkins University Press.

Leigh, Robert Adam. 2013. "On Theriac to Piso, Attributed to Galen. A critical edition with translation and commentary." PhD thesis, Department of Classics, Exeter.

Liebig, Justus. 1831. "Ueber einen neuen Apparat zur Analyse organischer Körper, und über die Zusarnmensetzung einiger organischer Substanzen." *Annalen der Physik und Chemie*: 1–42.

Lind, James. 1753. *Treatise on the Scurvy*. 2nd ed. Edinburgh: Sands, Murray and Cochran for A Kincaid and A Donaldson.

Mackie, John L. 1980. *The Cement of the Universe*. Oxford: Clarendon Press .

Marks, Harry M. 1997. *The Progress of Experiment: Science and Therapeutic Reform in the United States, 1900–1990*. Cambridge: Cambridge University Press.

Mayo, Deborah G. 1996. *Error and the Growth of Experimental Knowledge*. Chicago: The University of Chicago Press.

McVaugh, Michael. 2009. "The 'Experience-Based Medicine' of the Thirteenth Century." In *Evidence and Interpretation in Studies on Early Science and Medicine*, edited by Edith Sylla and William R. Newman, 105–130. Leiden: Brill.

Mill, John Stuart. 1843. *A System of Logic*. London: John W. Parker.

Miller, Stanley L. 1953. "A Production of Amino Acids under Possible Primitive Earth Conditions." *Science* 117 (3046): 528–529. https://doi.org/10.1126/science.117.3046.528.

1955. "Production of Some Organic Compounds under Possible Primitive Earth Conditions." *Journal of the American Chemical Society* 77 (9): 2351–2361. https://doi.org/10.1021/ja01614a001.

Miller, Stanley L., and Harold C. Urey. 1959. "Organic Compound Synthesis on the Primitive Earth." *Science* 130 (3370): 245–251. www.science.org/doi/abs/10.1126/science.130.3370.245.

Morabia, Alfredo. 2011. "History of the Modern Epidemiological Concept of Confounding." *Journal of Epidemiology and Community Health* 65: 297–300.

Morel, Laurence. 2004. "Mouse Models of Human Autoimmune Diseases: Essential Tools That Require the Proper Controls." *PLOS Biology* 2 (8): 1061–1064. e241. https://doi.org/10.1371/journal.pbio.0020241.

Nasser, Mona, Aida Tibi, and Emilie Savage-Smith. 2009. "Ibn Sina's Canon of Medicine: 11th Century Rules for Assessing the Effects of Drugs." *Journal of the Royal Society of Medicine* 102: 78–80.

Needham, John Turbervill. 1748. "A Summary of Some Late Observations upon the Generation, Composition, and Decomposition of Animal and Vegetable Substances; Communicated in a Letter to Martin Folkes, Esq.; President of the Royal Society, by Mr. Tubervill Needham, Fellow of the Same Society." *Philosophical Transactions of the Royal Society of London* 45: 615–666.

OECD Working Party on Good Laboratory Practice, GLP. 2022. *Advisory Document of the Working Party on Good Laboratory Practice on Quality Assurance and GLP.* OECD. https://one.oecd.org/document/env/cbc/mono(2022)20/en/pdf.

Oparin, Alexander I. 1938. *The Origin of Life*. New York: The Macmillan.

Overgaard, Morten. 2004. "Confounding Factors in Contrastive Analysis." *Synthese* 141 (2): 217–231. www.jstor.org/stable/20118477.

Parke, Emily C. 2014. "Flies from Meat and Wasps from Trees: Reevaluating Francesco Redi's Spontaneous Generation Experiments." *Studies in History and Philosophy of Biological and Biomedical Sciences* 45: 34–42.

Pauly, Philip J. 1987. *Controlling Life: Jacques Loeb & the Engineering Ideal in Biology.* Oxford: Oxford University Press.

Pearl, Judea, and Dana Mackenzie. 2020. *The Book of Why: The New Science of Cause and Effect*. New York: Basic Books. 2018.

Pence, Charles H. 2021. *The Causal Structure of Natural Selection*. Cambridge: Cambridge University Press.

Potochnik, Angela M., Matteo Colombo, and Cory Wright. 2019. *Recipes for Science: An Introduction to Scientific Methods and Reasoning*. New York: Routledge.

Prescott, F. 1930. "Spallanzani on Spontaneous Generation and Digestion: Life and Works of Spallanzani." *Proceedings of the Royal Society of Medicine* 23: 495–510.

"Principles of Refereeing." 2017. *Nature Cell Biology* 19: 1005.

Rader, Karen. 2004. *Making Mice: Standardizing Animals for American Biomedical Research*. Princeton: Princeton University Press.

Ratcliff, Marc. 2009. *The Quest for the Invisible: Microscopy in the Enlightenment*. Farnham: Ashgate.

Raynaud, Dominique. 2015. *Scientific Controversies: A Socio-Historical Perspective on the Advancement of Science*. New Brunswick: Transaction.

Redi, Francesco. 1909. *Experiments on the Generation of Insects*. Chicago: Open Court. 1688.

Reichenbach, Hans. 1956. *The Direction of Time*. Berkeley: University of California Press.

Rheinberger, Hans-Jörg. 2023. *Split and Splice: A Phenomenology of Experimentation*. Chicago: University of Chicago Press.

Roberts, William. 1874. "Studies on Biogenesis." *Transaction of the Royal Society* 164: 457–477.

Rozman, Ula, and Gabriela Kalčíková. 2022. "Seeking for a Perfect (Non-Spherical) Microplastic Particle – The Most Comprehensive Review on Microplastic Laboratory Research." *Journal of Hazardous Materials* 424: 1–17. www.sciencedirect.com/science/article/pii/S0304389421024973.

Safety Culture Content Team (2023) "A Guide to Good Laboratory Practice (GLP)." Accessed July 8, 2023. https://safetyculture.com/topics/good-laboratory-practice-glp/.

Sarzotti-Kelsoe, Marcella, Josephine Cox, Naana Cleland, et al. 2009. "Evaluation and Recommendations on Good Clinical Laboratory Practice Guidelines for Phase I-III Clinical Trials." *PLoS Medicine* 6 (5): 1–5. https://doi.org/10.1371/journal.pmed.1000067.

Schickore, Jutta. 2009. "Test Objects." *History of Science* 47: 117–145.

2017. *About Method : Experimenters, Snake Venom, and the History of Writing Scientifically*. Chicago: The University of Chicago Press.

2019. "The Structure and Function of Experimental Control in the Life Sciences." *Philosophy of Science* 86 (2): 203–218.

Schickore, Jutta, and William R. Newman, eds. 2024. *Elusive Phenomena, Unwieldy Things: Experimental Control in Historical Perspective*. Cham: Springer.

Schulze, Franz. 1836. "Vorläufige Mittheilung der Resultate einer experimentellen Beobachtung über Generatio aequivoca." *Annalen der Physik und Chemie* 39: 486–489.

Schürch, Caterina. 2024. "One Myrtle Proves Nothing: Repeated Comparative Experiments and the Growing Awareness of the Difficulty of Conducting Conclusive Experiments." In *Elusive Phenomena, Unwieldy Things:*

Historical Perspectives on Experimental Control, edited by Jutta Schickore and William R. Newman, 55–104. Cham: Springer.

Seppel, Marten, and Keith Tribe. 2017. *Cameralism in Practice: State Administration and Economy in Early Modern Europe*. Rochester: The Boydell Press.

Shapin, Steven, and Simon Schaffer. 1985. *Leviathan and the Air-Pump: Hobbes, Boyle, and the Experimental Life*. Princeton: Princeton University Press.

Sloan, Philip. 1992. "Organic Molecules Revisited." In *Buffon 88* edited by Jean-Claude Beaune and Jean Gayon: 415–438. Paris: J. Vrin.

Solomon, Miriam. 2022. "On Validators for Psychiatric Categories." *Philosophy of Medicine* 3 (1): 1–23.

Spallanzani, Lazzarro. 1803. *Tracts on the Natural History of Animals and Vegetables*. 2nd ed. Vol. 1. Edinburgh.

Stasinopoulos, Triant C., and Roger P. Hangarter. 1990. "Preventing Photochemistry in Culture Media by Long-Pass Light Filters Alters Growth of Cultured Tissues." *Plant Physiology* 93 (4): 1365–1369. https://doi.org/10.1104/pp.93.4.1365.

Steinle, Friedrich. 2005. *Explorative Experimente: Ampere, Faraday und die Ursprünge der Elektrodynamik*. Stuttgart: Franz Steiner Verlag.

Stigler, Stephen. 1974. "Gergonne's 1815 Paper on the Design and Analysis of Polynomial Regression Experiments." *Historia Mathematica* 1: 431–447.

Strick, James. 2000. *Sparks of Life: Darwinism and the Victorian Debates over Spontaneous Generation*. Cambridge: Harvard University Press.

2004. *The Origin of Life Debate: Cells, Molecules and Generation*. 6 Vols. Bristol: Thoemmes.

2009. "Spontaneous Generation." In *Encyclopedia of Microbiology*. 3rd ed., edited by Moselio Schaechter, 80–90. Oxford: Academic Press.

Sullivan, Jacqueline Anne. 2022. "Novel Tool Development and the Dynamics of Control: The Rodent Touchscreen Operant Chamber as a Case Study." *Philosophy of Science* 89 (5): 1–19.

Torday, John S., and František Baluška. 2019. "Why Control an Experiment?" *EMBO reports* 20 (10): 1–4. e49110. https://doi.org/10.15252/embr.201949110.

Treece, James W. 1990. "Daniel and the Classic Experimental Design." Accessed January 29, 2023. www.icr.org/article/daniel-classic-experimental-design.

Urey, Harold C. 1952. "On the Early Chemical History of the Earth and the Origin of Life." *Proceedings of the National Academy of Sciences* 38 (4): 351–363. https://doi.org/10.1073/pnas.38.4.351.

Wimsatt, William C. 2007. *Re-Engineering Philosophy for Limited Beings*. Cambridge: Harvard University Press.

Woodward, James. 2003a. "Experimentation, Causal Inference, and Instrumental Realism." In *Philosophy of Scientific Experimentation*, edited by Hans Radder, 87–118. Pittsburgh: Pittsburgh University Press.

2003b. *Making Things Happen: A Theory of Causal Explanation*. Oxford: Oxford University Press.

2008. "Cause and Explanation in Psychiatry: An Interventionist Perspective." In *Philosophical Issues in Psychiatry: Explanation, Phenomenology and Nosology*, edited by Kenneth S. Kendler and Josef Parnas. Baltimore: Johns Hopkins University Press.

Worrall, John. 2007. "Why There's No Cause to Randomize." *British Journal for the Philosophy of Science* 58: 451–488.

Wunsch, Guillaume. 2007. "Confounding and Control." *Demographic Research* 16 (4): 97–120.

Zhmud, Leonid. 2012. *Pythagoras and the Early Pythagoreans*. Oxford: Oxford University Press.

Cambridge Elements

The Philosophy of Biology

Grant Ramsey
KU Leuven

Grant Ramsey is a BOFZAP research professor at the Institute of Philosophy, KU Leuven, Belgium. His work centers on philosophical problems at the foundation of evolutionary biology. He has been awarded the Popper Prize twice for his work in this area. He also publishes in the philosophy of animal behavior, human nature and the moral emotions. He runs the Ramsey Lab (theramseylab.org), a highly collaborative research group focused on issues in the philosophy of the life sciences.

Michael Ruse
Florida State University

Michael Ruse is the Lucyle T. Werkmeister Professor of Philosophy and the Director of the Program in the History and Philosophy of Science at Florida State University. He is Professor Emeritus at the University of Guelph, in Ontario, Canada. He is a former Guggenheim fellow and Gifford lecturer. He is the author or editor of over sixty books, most recently *Darwinism as Religion: What Literature Tells Us about Evolution; On Purpose; The Problem of War: Darwinism, Christianity, and their Battle to Understand Human Conflict;* and *A Meaning to Life*.

About the Series

This Cambridge Elements series provides concise and structured introductions to all of the central topics in the philosophy of biology. Contributors to the series are cutting-edge researchers who offer balanced, comprehensive coverage of multiple perspectives, while also developing new ideas and arguments from a unique viewpoint.

Cambridge Elements

The Philosophy of Biology

Elements in the Series

A full series listing is available at: www.cambridge.org/EPBY

Printed in the United States
by Baker & Taylor Publisher Services